FLORIDA TRIVIA

REVISED EDITION

D1467042

FLORIDA TRIVIA

COMPILED BY
ERNIE & JILL COUCH

REVISED EDITION

Rutledge Hill Press®
Nashville, Tennessee

Published by Rutledge Hill Press, a Division of Thomas Nelson Inc., P.O.Box 141000, Nashville, Tennessee 37214.

Typography by D&T/Bailey, Nashville, Tennessee
Book and cover design by Ken Morris, M², Nashville, Tennessee

Library of Congress Cataloging-in-Publication Data

Couch, Ernie, 1949-
    Florida trivia / compiled by Ernie & Jill Couch.—Rev. ed.
      p. cm.
    ISBN 1-55853-316-8
    1. Florida—History—Miscellanea. 2. Questions and answers.
I. Couch, Jill, 1948-   .   II. Title
F311.5.C68   1994   94-32152
975.9—dc20   CIP

Printed in the United States of America
1 2 3 4 5 - 08 07 06 05 04

PREFACE

Conversations about the state of Florida are likely to include such topics as beaches, sunshine, palm trees, theme parks, and oranges. Yet those images of the Sunshine State can seem superficial when compared to its fascinating and multifaceted character. Florida is comprised of a richly diversified land and people with colorful traditions and a compelling history. Captured within these pages are some of the highlights of this rich heritage, both the known and the not-so-well known.

In the eight years since *Florida Trivia* was first published, current information has changed, new events have brought about new questions, and some errors in the first edition have been gently pointed out to us. This revised and updated edition incorporates those sorts of changes, and includes more than seventy-five new trivia questions.

Florida Trivia is designed to be informative, educational, and entertaining. But most of all, we hope that reading these pages will inspire you to learn more about the great state of Florida.

Ernie & Jill Couch

To
Mamie and Berry E. Couch
and
the great people of Florida

TABLE OF CONTENTS

GEOGRAPHY

C H A P T E R   O N E

Q. What is the most densely populated county in Florida?

A. Pinellas, with 2,000 persons per square mile.

———◆———

Q. What town was named for a variety of tobacco?

A. Sumatra.

———◆———

Q. Where do the Everglades rank in size among the other U.S. national parks?

A. Third.

———◆———

Q. How many counties does Florida have?

A. Sixty-seven.

———◆———

Q. Because of its expensive shops and wealthy clientele, what street in Palm Beach is one of the most famous in the world?

A. Worth Avenue.

Q. What states border Florida?

A. Georgia and Alabama.

———◆———

Q. How many miles separate Key West from Cuba?

A. Ninety.

———◆———

Q. The town Eustis has been called by what two other names?

A. Highlands and Pendryville.

———◆———

Q. What is the geographic center of the state?

A. Hernando, twelve miles north-northwest of Brooksville.

———◆———

Q. In 1992, Hurricane Andrew virtually leveled what city?

A. Homestead (and the Homestead Air Force Base).

———◆———

Q. In what city is the St. Vincent de Paul Seminary?

A. Boynton Beach.

———◆———

Q. What inhospitable swamp covers a large part of Franklin County?

A. Tate's Hell Swamp.

Q. "Stick of fire" is the Indian meaning for what city's name?

A. Tampa.

———◆———

Q. What community supplies most of the houseplants Florida produces?

A. Apopka.

———◆———

Q. For what English town was Avon Park named?

A. Stratford-on-Avon.

———◆———

Q. On what key were sixty-one pieces of gold unearthed in 1911?

A. Grassy Key.

———◆———

Q. What is the major industry of Brooksville?

A. Quarrying and distribution of limestone.

———◆———

Q. Thousands of letters are sent to what town each year because of its unusual postmark?

A. Christmas.

———◆———

Q. How many municipalities does Dade County contain?

A. Twenty-seven.

Q. Florida has how many public and private airports?

A. Approximately 455.

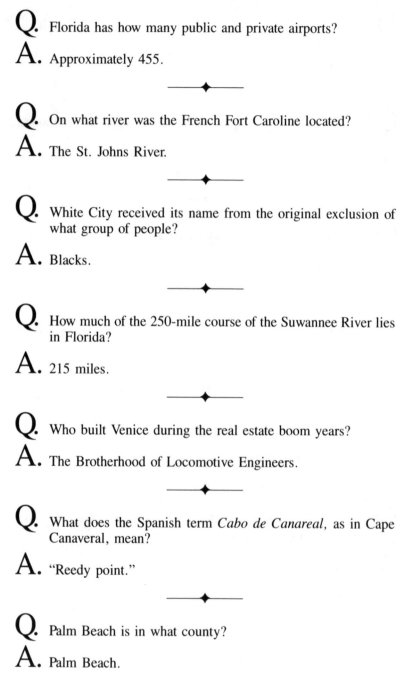

Q. On what river was the French Fort Caroline located?

A. The St. Johns River.

Q. White City received its name from the original exclusion of what group of people?

A. Blacks.

Q. How much of the 250-mile course of the Suwannee River lies in Florida?

A. 215 miles.

Q. Who built Venice during the real estate boom years?

A. The Brotherhood of Locomotive Engineers.

Q. What does the Spanish term *Cabo de Canareal,* as in Cape Canaveral, mean?

A. "Reedy point."

Q. Palm Beach is in what county?

A. Palm Beach.

Q. What type of organization is Lake Como in Lutz?

A. A nudist colony.

Q. How much of the area of Fort Lauderdale is water?

A. One-tenth (165 miles of navigable water).

Q. Magnificent estates and dazzling hotels line what major thoroughfare in Miami Beach?

A. Collins Avenue.

Q. Where in 1521 did Ponce de León attempt to establish a colony?

A. In the vicinity of Charlotte Harbor.

Q. The Bill Baggs Cape Florida State Park, complete with an early nineteenth-century lighthouse, is on what Florida island?

A. Key Biscayne.

Q. By what name is State Road 405 known where it leaves the mainland for Merritt Island?

A. NASA Parkway.

Q. What group owns and operates the 316,000-acre Desert Ranch west of Melbourne?

A. The Mormons.

Q. How many miles of coastline give Florida the longest tidal coast of any state in the contiguous United States?

A. 8,462.

Q. In the Florida Keys, mile markers along the overseas highway are often used for what purpose other than indicating distance from Key West?

A. As addresses.

Q. What community is known as the "City Way Down upon the Suwannee River"?

A. Cross City.

Q. How many artesian springs are there in Florida?

A. Twenty-seven.

Q. What portion of the Everglades is nearest the west coast?

A. The Big Cypress Swamp.

Q. Ringling Clown College is in what town?

A. Venice.

Q. Where on the Florida Reef was Fort Jefferson constructed in the mid-1880s?

A. The Dry Tortugas.

Q. What is the southernmost city of the continental United States?

A. Key West.

Q. What Florida spring is one of the nation's deepest?

A. The main spring of Wakulla Springs (explored to 250 feet).

Q. Melbourne and what other community merged in 1969?

A. Eau Gallie.

Q. Where is the dividing line between the subtropical and tropical climates in Florida?

A. Subtropical is north of Bradenton-Lake Okeechobee-Vero Beach and tropical is south of it.

Q. The Tamiami Trail is named for what two cities situated at each end of this highway?

A. Tampa and Miami.

Q. Joseph W. Young and his California associates founded what town in 1921?

A. Hollywood.

Q. What present-day ghost town possessed Florida's largest population in 1838?

A. St. Joseph.

Q. What ocean forms the eastern border of Florida?

A. The Atlantic.

Q. What town is named for a large Australian city?

A. Melbourne.

Q. In 1860, what island became the terminus of Florida's first cross-state railroad and, consequently, the state's first resort?

A. Amelia Island.

Q. What community was settled by Polish families in 1912?

A. Korona.

Q. What city is known as the "Sponge Capital of America"?

A. Tarpon Springs.

Q. In 1905, what religious group founded a relatively short-lived commune near Alligator Lake?

A. The Shakers.

Q. W. J. Howey established what community in 1916 as the center of his vast citrus-growing empire?

A. Howey-in-the-Hills.

Q. What was the name of the Palatka home and estate of Judge Isaac H. Bronson that was occupied alternately by Union and Confederate troops during the Civil War?

A. Mullholland Place.

Q. What was the former name of Haines City?

A. Clay Cut.

Q. Originally founded as Lakeview and later renamed Osceola, what is the present name of this college town?

A. Winter Park.

Q. What was chosen as the best beach in the United States for 1994 by the Laboratory for Coastal Research?

A. Grayton Beach State Recreational Area.

Q. Who sold twenty-six million dollars' worth of real estate lots in Boca Raton?

A. Addison Mizner.

Q. By what name is Walt Disney World called in the Florida statutes?

A. The Reedy Creek Improvement District.

Q. The community of Oldsmar, which later was renamed Tampa Shores, was founded in 1916 by what automobile manufacturer?

A. R. E. Olds.

Q. What Florida coast is known as the Gold Coast?

A. The east coast.

———————◆———————

Q. What 825-foot manmade promontory extends into the Atlantic at Cocoa Beach?

A. Canaveral Pier.

———————◆———————

Q. In what city is the state capitol situated?

A. Tallahassee.

———————◆———————

Q. Where did Jackie Kennedy and her children seek privacy following the assassination of President Kennedy?

A. Jupiter Island.

———————◆———————

Q. What is the greatest distance between the northern and southern borders of Florida?

A. 447 miles (719 kilometers).

———————◆———————

Q. What city is home of the famous Orange Bowl?

A. Miami.

———————◆———————

Q. The water tower in what city is topped by a 55-foot high, 37-foot wide strawberry?

A. Plant City.

Q. Florida's west coast from Tampa Bay south to the Everglades is aptly called by what nickname?

A. "The Suncoast."

———◆———

Q. The county courthouse in what town is styled after Thomas Jefferson's noted home?

A. Monticello.

———◆———

Q. What town calls itself the "Tree Capital of the South"?

A. Perry.

———◆———

Q. What partially completed fort is situated on the northern end of Amelia Island?

A. Fort Clinch.

———◆———

Q. Where have the oldest Indian projectile points been found in the state?

A. Warm Springs near Venice.

———◆———

Q. How many Native Americans live on reservations in Florida?

A. 36,335.

———◆———

Q. For whom was Fort Lauderdale named during the Seminole Wars?

A. Maj. William Lauderdale of Tennessee.

Q. Near what town in the early 1900s did Japanese settlers found the Yamato Colony, a farming community?

A. Delray Beach.

———◆———

Q. What name did the Spanish originally give Key West?

A. Caya Hueso, meaning "Island of Bones."

———◆———

Q. What does the name *Kissimmee* mean in the Calusa Indian language?

A. "Heaven's Place."

———◆———

Q. By what two previous names was Milton known?

A. Scratch Ankle and Hard Scrabble.

———◆———

Q. The University of Miami is situated in what city?

A. Coral Gables.

———◆———

Q. What name was originally given to Miami Inlet by the English?

A. Dartmouth Inlet.

———◆———

Q. By what name is the slow-moving freshwater river fifty miles wide and a few inches deep, fed by Lake Okeechobee, known?

A. The Everglades.

Q. What is the largest island of the Florida Keys?

A. Key Largo.

---◆---

Q. What are the three main land regions of Florida?

A. The Atlantic Coastal Plain, the East Gulf Coastal Plain, and the Florida Uplands.

---◆---

Q. John Milton, governor during the Civil War, is buried in the churchyard cemetery of the St. Luke's Episcopal Church of what town?

A. Marianna.

---◆---

Q. How many subtropical islands make up the Florida Keys?

A. Forty-three.

---◆---

Q. What is Charlotte County's only incorporated community?

A. Punta Gorda.

---◆---

Q. What name did John Ringling give his mansion in Sarasota?

A. Ca'd'zan, Italian for "House of John."

---◆---

Q. The Apalachicola National Forest covers sections of how many counties?

A. Four (Franklin, Leon, Liberty, and Wakulla).

Q. What three nicknames have been given to Florida?

A. "Sunshine State," "Peninsula State," and "Everglade State."

Q. What name was given to the channel constructed from the Indian River to Mosquito Lagoon?

A. The Haulover.

Q. What promoter gave Pensacola the title "the Naples of Florida"?

A. W. D. Chipley.

Q. What community received the nickname "Millionaires' Colony"?

A. Ormond Beach.

Q. What is the greatest distance between the eastern and western borders of Florida?

A. 361 miles (581 kilometers).

Q. What is the name of the 240-foot observation tower at Lake Placid?

A. Happiness Tower.

Q. Where on Jacksonville Beach may the flags of all fifty states be viewed?

A. The Flag Pavilion.

Q. In what county is the community of Two Egg?

A. Jackson County.

———◆———

Q. Miami's garment district, the nation's second largest, has approximately how many manufacturers?

A. Five hundred.

———◆———

Q. What town serves as the shipping point for Indian River Citrus Fruits?

A. Cocoa.

———◆———

Q. How high into the air is Jacksonville's Friendship Fountain capable of spraying water?

A. Up to 120 feet.

———◆———

Q. What nature area is within the city limits of Fort Pierce?

A. The Savannahs Wilderness Area.

———◆———

Q. Who started development of Miami Beach in 1915?

A. Carl Fisher.

———◆———

Q. What Florida military installation is the largest air force base in the world?

A. Eglin Field.

Q. What is Florida's rank in land area among all the states?

A. Twenty-second.

———————◆———————

Q. Where may the eighteen-foot John F. Kennedy Memorial Torch of Friendship be seen?

A. Bayfront Park, Miami.

———————◆———————

Q. What river marks the western boundary of the Ocala National Forest?

A. Oklawaha River.

———————◆———————

Q. Who founded Daytona Beach?

A. Mathias Day.

———————◆———————

Q. What city, and its beachfront, has become a traditional gathering place for college students on spring break?

A. Fort Lauderdale.

———————◆———————

Q. Dunedin in Pinellas County is filled primarily with peoples from what ethnic background?

A. Scottish.

———————◆———————

Q. What is the longest continuous bridge in Florida?

A. Seven Mile Bridge in the Florida Keys.

Q. What city is called the "Cigar Capital of the United States"?

A. Tampa.

———◆———

Q. What two communities merged with Panama City in 1909?

A. St. Andrews and Millville.

———◆———

Q. What was the name of the retirement community built by J. C. Penney for pastors of all denominations near Green Cove Springs?

A. Penney Farms Memorial Home Community.

———◆———

Q. By what name was Lamont originally called?

A. Lick Skillet.

———◆———

Q. What town was first called Newton when founded by South Carolina planters in 1838?

A. Madison.

———◆———

Q. In 1909, many veterans of the Grand Army of the Republic settled in what town?

A. St. Cloud.

———◆———

Q. What is the meaning of the name of the town of Islamorada on Matecumbe Island?

A. "Purple Island," because of purple-colored snails in nearby waters.

Q. What is the predominantly Cuban area of southwestern Miami called?

A. Little Havana.

Q. What community was originally known as Wisconsin Settlement because of its founding in the 1870s by families from Eau Claire, Wisconsin?

A. Orange City.

Q. What river is the largest in the state?

A. The St. Johns River, in northeast Florida.

Q. Where is the one major bay on the eastern coast?

A. Biscayne Bay.

Q. Florida public school integration, enacted in 1959, first took place in what county?

A. Dade.

Q. What name has been given to the islets that fringe the lower Gulf coast of Florida?

A. Ten Thousand Islands.

Q. Who was the first known white man to establish residence in the area of Safety Harbor at the head of Old Tampa Bay in 1823?

A. Odet Philippe.

Q. What plasticware company, known for its ability to lock in freshness, is headquartered in Kissimmee?

A. Tupperware International.

------◆------

Q. Who was the Japanese industrialist who gave a Japanese garden and teahouse to Miami in 1961?

A. Kiyoshi Ishimura.

------◆------

Q. The northern section of the Everglades is known by what name?

A. The Okaloacoochee Slough.

------◆------

Q. Monument Island, with its ninety-six-foot column, honors what late-nineteenth-century developer and railroad magnate?

A. Henry Flagler.

------◆------

Q. In what county is the Crystal River State Archeological Site situated?

A. Citrus County.

------◆------

Q. Florida's shoreline has approximately how many miles of beaches?

A. Eight hundred.

------◆------

Q. The greater Orlando area includes portions of what three counties?

A. Orange, Seminole, and Osceola.

Q. What three major bays are on the Gulf coast?

A. Charlotte Harbor, Sarasota, and Tampa.

———◆———

Q. Indian River is what type of body of water?

A. A long, narrow lagoon.

———◆———

Q. What is the northernmost main island in the Florida Keys?

A. Key Largo.

———◆———

Q. What city has the largest land area of any city in Florida?

A. Jacksonville.

———◆———

Q. What county leads Florida in petroleum production?

A. Santa Rosa.

———◆———

Q. The Emerald Coast describes what strip of coastline?

A. The area from Destin to Ft. Walton Beach, part of the Panhandle.

———◆———

Q. What town in St. Lucie County was settled by Danish immigrants from Chicago?

A. White City.

Q. How many bridges connect the Florida Keys?

A. Forty-two.

———◆———

Q. What river forms an approximately fifty-mile-long boundary between Florida and Alabama?

A. The Perdido.

———◆———

Q. What term is used to refer to a person born and bred on Key West?

A. "Conch."

———◆———

Q. Horse farms in what county are noted for their Thoroughbred racing stock?

A. Marion.

———◆———

Q. Wauchula, the seat of Hardee County, has what Indian meaning?

A. "Sandhill crane."

———◆———

Q. What university was named for a hat manufacturer?

A. Stetson University in De Land.

———◆———

Q. By what name did the Indians of the Caribbean call Florida?

A. Bimini.

Q. What was the name of the narrow-gauge railroad that connected the community of Jupiter with the communities of Neptune, Mars, Venus, and Juno?

A. The Celestial Railroad.

Q. Hawk's Cay, a luxurious resort, is on what key?

A. Duck Key.

Q. What name did Ponce de León first give Florida?

A. The Isle of Flowers.

Q. What river flows through Tampa?

A. Hillsborough River.

Q. When Pinellas County was formed in 1912, what town became the county seat?

A. Clearwater.

Q. In what city were bars first built to let cowboys get a drink without having to dismount from their horses?

A. Kissimmee.

Q. De Funiak Springs is the seat of what county?

A. Walton.

Q. What city proclaims itself "the Venice of America"?

A. Fort Lauderdale.

———◆———

Q. Who was the baking powder manufacturer who formed a town in Volusia County that bears his name?

A. Henry A. De Land.

———◆———

Q. What name did the Spanish give to Amelia Island?

A. Santa Maria.

———◆———

Q. By 1981, how many businesses in Dade County were owned or operated by Cubans?

A. Approximately 18,000.

———◆———

Q. What exclusive community sits on the north end of the new Miami Beach?

A. Bal Harbour.

———◆———

Q. What is the largest city in the Florida Panhandle?

A. Pensacola.

———◆———

Q. What community is known as the "City with the Mile Long Mall"?

A. Avon Park.

Q. The State Archives, Museum of Florida History, and State Library are in what Tallahassee building?

A. R. A. Gray Building.

Q. What group changed the name of Utica to Bowling Green in the 1880s?

A. Farm settlers from Bowling Green, Kentucky.

Q. What town on Lake Tsala Apopka was named for a town in Scotland?

A. Inverness.

Q. In what community did Populist party leader Lonnie Weeks live from 1892–1912?

A. Bonifay.

Q. Cudjoe Key is a contraction of what name?

A. Cousin Joe's.

Q. What community near Maitland became one of the first incorporated black towns in the nation in the late 1880s?

A. Eatonville.

Q. For what was Fruitland Park named by Maj. O. P. Rooks in 1876?

A. The Fruitland Nurseries of Augusta, Georgia.

Q. In what town is the Florida Cattlemen's Association situated?

A. Kissimmee.

Q. Where may a grave be found in the middle of the street?

A. Canova Street in New Smyrna.

Q. What community was originally named Indian River City in 1882?

A. Cocoa.

Q. What sugar mill headquartered in Clewiston is the south's largest?

A. United States Sugar Corporation.

Q. After what structure in Venice, Italy, did John Ringling pattern his mansion in Sarasota?

A. Doge's Palace.

Q. What settlement is the oldest in the Miami area?

A. Coconut Grove.

Q. The highest point of elevation in Florida is found in what county?

A. Walton County, 345 feet (105 meters) above sea level.

Q. What span of road and bridge was opened across Tampa Bay in 1954?

A. The Sunshine Skyway.

———◆———

Q. In whose honor was Fernandina named?

A. Dom Domingo Fernándina.

———◆———

Q. On how many pilings does the Seven Mile Bridge in the Florida Keys sit?

A. 544.

———◆———

Q. What was the first incorporated city on the Pinellas Keys?

A. Pass-a-Grille Beach.

———◆———

Q. Who founded Polk City in 1922?

A. Isaac Van Horn.

———◆———

Q. Before 1859, Lake City was known by what reptile name in honor of a local Seminole chief?

A. Alligator.

———◆———

Q. Who built the Tampa Bay Hotel, in which the University of Tampa's administrative offices are now situated?

A. Henry B. Plant.

Q. What is the distance from Key West to the Dry Tortugas?

A. Sixty-eight miles.

————◆————

Q. What name did Ponce de León give to Cape Canaveral in 1513?

A. Cape of Currents.

————◆————

Q. What historical event is credited for allowing Miami to become a resort community?

A. Henry Flagler brought his railroad to Miami in 1896.

————◆————

Q. What beach claims to be the "world's safest beach"?

A. New Smyrna Beach.

————◆————

Q. Who was the Russian railroad czar who founded St. Petersburg?

A. Peter Demens.

————◆————

Q. Jacksonville covers how many square miles?

A. 841.

————◆————

Q. What Florida river is one of the few rivers in the world that flows north?

A. The St. Johns River.

Q. How many acres are contained in the Collier-Seminole State Park?

A. 6,423.

———◆———

Q. The Church of Scientology has offices in what former hotel in Clearwater?

A. The Fort Harrison.

———◆———

Q. What house is Pensacola's oldest?

A. The Widow Troulett House.

———◆———

Q. By what name did the British call a St. Johns River cattle crossing that became the city of Jacksonville?

A. Cow Ford.

———◆———

Q. What area was noted as a supplier of wood to manufacture pencils?

A. Cedar Key.

———◆———

Q. What fashionable spa did President Grover Cleveland visit?

A. Green Cove Springs.

———◆———

Q. Over what Florida town did the Mexican flag fly for a short time in 1817?

A. Fernandina.

Q. Which building at the Kennedy Space Center is 716 feet long, 588 feet wide, and 525 feet high?

A. The Vehicle Assembly Building.

Q. What name did Ponce de León give the Florida Keys?

A. The Martyrs.

Q. What city is the world's largest cruise port?

A. Miami.

Q. By what name is the land lying north of Lake Okeechobee known?

A. The Kissimmee Prairies.

Q. How large is Florida in square miles?

A. 58,560 square miles (151,679 square kilometers), including inland water but excluding 1,735 square miles (4,494 square kilometers) of coastal water.

Q. Who was the designer of the first yacht basins at Hollywood who already had gained fame as the chief engineer of the Panama Canal?

A. Gen. George Washington Goethals.

Q. Measuring a mere eight feet, four inches by seven feet, three inches, where is the nation's smallest post office?

A. Ochopee.

Q. What kind of land mass did the first European explorers believe Florida to be?

A. An island.

———◆———

Q. What two great business figures purchased property in the Green Cove Springs area and aided in its development?

A. Gail Borden and J. C. Penney.

———◆———

Q. What is the name of the world's oldest airline, which is based in Miami?

A. Chalk's Flying Service.

———◆———

Q. The name of the Suwannee River is a corruption of what original Spanish name?

A. San Juanee ("little St. Johns").

———◆———

Q. Where was President Richard M. Nixon's Florida White House?

A. Key Biscayne.

———◆———

Q. What is the area of Lake Okeechobee?

A. 717 square miles.

———◆———

Q. How many federal Indian reservations are in Florida?

A. Four.

Q. Near what present-day site was Calusa Indian Chief Chekika hanged in 1840 after attacking Indian Key?

A. Chekika State Park, near Homestead.

———◆———

Q. In what time zone is the western part of the Panhandle?

A. Central.

———◆———

Q. What is the length of the Howard Frankland Bridge across Tampa Bay?

A. 15,872 feet.

———◆———

Q. What community was the seat of old Dade County from 1889 to 1891?

A. Juno.

———◆———

Q. What site had become a popular resort for residents of Tampa by the early 1900s?

A. Indian Rocks.

———◆———

Q. What community was named by Italian laborers who worked on the construction of the Atlantic Coast Line?

A. Zolfo Springs.

———◆———

Q. What is the meaning of the Indian word *pilaklikaha* from which the name of Palatka in Putnam County is derived?

A. "Crossing over."

Q. The layout of what Florida town was based on the mythological Greek city of Heliopolis?

A. Sebring.

Q. What is the northernmost lake in the sandy Florida ridge section of the state?

A. Kingsley Lake.

Q. What name was given to an enclave of racially mixed persons in the area of Ponce de León, dating to the early 1860s?

A. Dominickers.

Q. What town has a growing Mennonite community?

A. Ellenton.

Q. What was the previous name of Indian River City?

A. Clark's Corner.

Q. The Florida Forest Service Nursery was relocated from Raiford to what town in 1928?

A. Sanderson.

Q. What community for employees with tuberculosis was established in 1875 by the Corbin Lock Company of New Britain, Connecticut?

A. Ormond, originally New Britain.

Q. What is the world's largest formation of clear artesian springs?

A. Silver Springs.

Q. For whom was the town of Bayard named by railroad magnate Henry M. Flagler?

A. Thomas F. Bayard.

Q. Archer, named for Confederate Brig. Gen. James J. Archer, was originally known by what name?

A. Deer Hammock.

Q. Where did Col. Elijah Clarke engage the British in battle on June 30, 1778?

A. On Alligator Creek, near Callahan.

Q. What is buried in the forty-two-foot-high manmade hill at Greynolds Park in the Miami area?

A. Rusted machinery.

Q. What community was named for the first president of Czecho-slovakia?

A. Masaryktown, for Tomas G. Masaryk.

Q. Eau Gallie is made from a French word and an Indian word meaning what?

A. "Rocky water."

Q. What is the second largest city in the state?

A. Miami.

———◆———

Q. What is the altitude of Iron Mountain?

A. 324 feet above sea level.

———◆———

Q. Fort Myers serves as the western terminus of what canal?

A. The Cross-State Canal.

———◆———

Q. The Rev. Edmund Snyder from Germantown, Pennsylvania, founded what community in 1885?

A. Okahumpka.

———◆———

Q. Dunedin was originally called by what name?

A. Jonesboro.

———◆———

Q. The port of Tampa handled how much tonnage in 1991?

A. 49.5 million.

———◆———

Q. What was the name of the Indian village that stood near present-day Mandarin?

A. Thimagua.

Q. What community became well known as the playground of the wealthy?

A. Palm Beach.

Q. What was the name of Taft in Orange County prior to 1909?

A. Smithville.

Q. What city constructed more hotel rooms between 1945 and 1954 than all of the rest of the state combined?

A. Miami.

Q. What town straddles the Florida–Alabama state line?

A. Flomaton.

Q. What is the meaning of the Indian term *Sopchoppy*, which is the name of a community and a river?

A. "Red oak."

Q. What planner of Gary, Indiana, founded Yankeetown in 1905?

A. Judge A. F. Knotts.

Q. Hilliard was first established for what purpose?

A. A trading post.

Q. What large body of water forms the western coast of Florida?

A. The Gulf of Mexico.

———◆———

Q. According to the Florida Division of Water Resources, what is the estimated number of lakes scattered throughout the state?

A. Approximately 30,000.

———◆———

Q. Flagler College is in what city?

A. St. Augustine.

———◆———

Q. How many miles of coastline separate Fort Lauderdale from Palm Beach?

A. Forty-five.

———◆———

Q. What is the meaning of the Indian word for which Lake Okeechobee is named?

A. "Big water."

———◆———

Q. What community was originally built on the causeway of the Overseas Highway?

A. Craig.

———◆———

Q. Where did the community of Wabasso get its name?

A. From Ossabaw Island in Georgia (spelled backwards).

ENTERTAINMENT

C H A P T E R   T W O

Q. Who led the first official visitor into the Magic Kingdom at Walt Disney World in 1971?

A. Mickey Mouse.

Q. What was the name of the eleventh James Bond movie, shot in St. Lucie and Marion counties in 1978–79?

A. *Moonraker.*

Q. What country music performer and songwriter was born in Pahokee on August 8, 1932?

A. Mel Tillis.

Q. What loincloth-clad movie star filmed several Tarzan movies at Silver Springs?

A. Johnny Weissmuller.

Q. What great entertainer attended the Florida School for the Deaf and Blind at St. Augustine?

A. Ray Charles.

Q. What Tampa-born musician took up a wind instrument as a child after a bout with polio and as an adult accompanied such stars as Stevie Wonder, Paul Simon, and David Bowie?

A. David William ("Dave") Sanborn.

◆

Q. What event is the largest night parade in the world?

A. The King Orange Jamboree Parade on New Year's Eve, Miami.

◆

Q. What March competition in Key West tests the ability to play a natural object as a musical instrument?

A. The Conch Shell Blowing Contest.

◆

Q. *Smokey and the Bandit II,* shot in Dade and Palm Beach counties and starring Jackie Gleason and Burt Reynolds, featured what actor in the role of Doc?

A. Dom DeLuise.

◆

Q. How many magical lands are in the Magic Kingdom at Disney World?

A. Seven.

◆

Q. What music festival is held at Arcadia?

A. Peace River Bluegrass Festival.

◆

Q. What attraction near Silver Springs brings the Wild West to life again?

A. Six Gun Territory.

Q. In what town do many carnival show people spend the winter?

A. Gibsonton.

———◆———

Q. What 1960 motion picture is given credit for depicting Fort Lauderdale as the place for college students to be on spring break?

A. *Where the Boys Are.*

———◆———

Q. What world famous precision-flying team is stationed at Sherman Field near Warrington?

A. The Blue Angels.

———◆———

Q. Flipper, the famous television porpoise, found a home in what Miami area attraction?

A. Seaquarium.

———◆———

Q. What kind of entertainment was first provided to Key Largo in 1980?

A. A movie theater.

———◆———

Q. What classic Marx Brothers movie was built around Florida's boom years of the 1920s?

A. *Cocoanuts.*

———◆———

Q. What outdoor drama depicting the trials and tragedies of early explorers Menéndez and Ribaut is presented in St. Augustine each summer?

A. *Cross and Sword.*

Q. In what city is the Florida State Fair held annually?

A. Tampa.

———◆———

Q. What country music singer and guitarist was born in McLellan?

A. Hank Locklin.

———◆———

Q. The houseboat used in what 1960s television series is anchored at Mallory Pier in Key West?

A. "Surfside 6."

———◆———

Q. What Miami-born entertainer gained fame as a singer with the rock group Blondie?

A. Deborah Harry.

———◆———

Q. What beauty pageant was presented as a television special from Dade County in 1985?

A. The Miss Teen USA Pageant.

———◆———

Q. Treasure Island is noted for the construction of what type of structures?

A. The world's largest sand castles.

———◆———

Q. What pre-Gator Bowl event in Jacksonville features live country and western entertainment?

A. Showdown Hoedown.

Q. What nationally known southern gospel quartet is headquartered in Pensacola?

A. The Florida Boys.

———◆———

Q. The World Showcase Plaza, a section of EPCOT, features what type of structures?

A. The world's most famous landmark buildings.

———◆———

Q. What group performs Broadway musicals in Panama City for ten weeks each summer?

A. The Florida State University Summer Music Theatre.

———◆———

Q. While working together in Miami, Harry Wayne ("H. W.") Casey and Rick Finch formed what rock group?

A. K. C. & the Sunshine Band.

———◆———

Q. Potter's Wax Museum in St. Augustine contains the likenesses of how many famous people?

A. More than 240.

———◆———

Q. What movie, filmed in Broward County in 1979, starred Chevy Chase, Bill Murray, Ted Knight, and Rodney Dangerfield?

A. *Caddyshack.*

———◆———

Q. Stuart was the birthplace of what musician who played with Jackie Wilson and such groups as the Drifters and the Platters?

A. Jack Arthur Walrath.

Q. What term was developed by Florida blacks in the early twentieth century to describe dance halls?

A. Juke joint.

Q. Orlando was the birthplace of what actress who played in "Designing Women"?

A. Delta Burke.

Q. What St. Petersburg-born jazz trombonist worked with Lionel Hampton, Benny Goodman, and Duke Ellington?

A. George ("Buster") Cooper.

Q. What giant water theme park is situated in the Hollywood–Fort Lauderdale area?

A. Six Flags Atlantis.

Q. Where is the "Spirit of Suwannee" Bluegrass Festival held?

A. Live Oak.

Q. What rodeo is Florida's oldest?

A. All-Florida Championship Rodeo at Arcadia.

Q. What 1942 novel by Robert Wilder gave rise to a prime time television soap opera?

A. "Flamingo Road."

Q. What is the name of the twisting roller coaster at Busch Gardens in Tampa?

A. The Python.

Q. Martin Bregman Productions produced part of what 1983 mobster movie filmed in Dade County?

A. *Scarface.*

Q. What two historical figures guide visitors through America's history in the American Adventure, World Showcase, EPCOT?

A. Benjamin Franklin and Mark Twain.

Q. Known for his relaxed singing style, what television personality has a home in the exclusive Jupiter Inlet Colony?

A. Perry Como.

Q. Where may a collection of more than 1,200 music machines be seen?

A. Bellms Cars and Music of Yesterday in Sarasota.

Q. What classic movie, starring Lauren Bacall, Humphrey Bogart, and Edward G. Robinson, was built around the story of a hurricane sweeping the Florida Keys?

A. *Key Largo.*

Q. What Pensacola-born actress appeared on the television series "Too Close for Comfort"?

A. Nancy Dussault.

Q. What native-born Florida actor, still a resident, convinced TV producers to film his 1994 series "Thunder in Paradise" in his home state?

A. Hulk Hogan.

———◆———

Q. Fidel Castro's ban on Christmas celebrations in Cuba brought about the 1972 inauguration of what annual Cuban-American festival in Miami?

A. The Three Kings Parade.

———◆———

Q. Where may a person ride the Gold Coast Railway?

A. Fort Lauderdale.

———◆———

Q. A boulevard in Miami is named for what television and movie personality who starred in the television series "The Honeymooners"?

A. Jackie Gleason.

———◆———

Q. What Miami-born entertainer was lead singer with Clara Ward from 1947–58?

A. Marion Williams.

———◆———

Q. Where in the Miami area may a person find bird shows, free-flying macaws, and marching flamingos?

A. Parrot Jungle.

———◆———

Q. In 1980, portions of what soap opera were shot in Broward County?

A. "Guiding Light."

Q. What Miami-born actor, singer, and dancer created the role of Chicken George in the 1977 television miniseries "Roots"?

A. Ben Vereen.

Q. Filmed in Palm Beach County, what 1981 movie starred Kathleen Turner as a wife trying to have her rich husband, played by Richard Crenna, murdered?

A. *Body Heat.*

Q. What was the name of Jimmy Buffett's band?

A. The Coral Reefer Band.

Q. Why was the first Silver Spurs Rodeo held at Kissimmee in 1944?

A. To benefit war bond sales.

Q. What contest is held annually at Spring Hill?

A. The Annual World Chicken-Plucking Contest.

Q. What world famous attraction at Walt Disney World features bears singing country music?

A. Country Bear Jamboree.

Q. St. Petersburg was the location of what 1979 motion picture in which a convention elected a president from candidates Lauren Bacall and Glenda Jackson?

A. *Health.*

Q. What four-ton killer whale is the star of the show at Sea World in Orlando?

A. Shamu.

Q. B. B. King selected what Pensacola native as one of his ten favorite guitarists?

A. Lloyd Ellis.

Q. What community is home for the Burt Reynolds Dinner Theatre?

A. Jupiter.

Q. Busch Gardens in Tampa follows an African theme and is known by what descriptive name?

A. The Dark Continent.

Q. What Miami-born actor won an Academy Award in 1963 for Best Actor in *Lilies of the Field*?

A. Sidney Poitier.

Q. What Pensacola-born newscaster became correspondent and co-anchor of the CBS Morning News?

A. Bill Kurtis.

Q. What Jacksonville-born trumpeter/singer was a regular member of Mort Lindsey's orchestra on the "Merv Griffin Show"?

A. Jack Sheldon.

Q. What seventeen-story sphere begins the adventure into Future World at EPCOT?

A. Spaceship Earth.

Q. Country music performer Slim Whitman was born in what Florida city on January 20, 1924?

A. Tampa.

Q. Florida's biggest traditional-style roller coaster is found at what attraction?

A. Circus World.

Q. What radio and TV personality married his "Jacksonville Jaguar" in 1994, the third marriage for each?

A. Rush Limbaugh married Marta Fitzgerald, a former University of North Florida student.

Q. In 1914, what city was called the "World's Winter Film Capital" because so many movie troupes were attracted there?

A. Jacksonville.

Q. What Marianna-born singer/songwriter received the 1968 Song of the Year Award for "Honey" from the Country Music Association?

A. Bobby Goldsboro.

Q. Where is the world's biggest All-Night Gospel Singing held?

A. Bonifay.

Q. When did Florida's first TV station begin broadcasting?

A. 1949 (WTVJ, Miami).

◆

Q. In what 1977 science fiction movie, shot in St. Lucie County, do giant ants invade a Florida coastal resort?

A. *Empire of the Ants.*

◆

Q. The training of what world-renowned show horses may be watched each winter in Sarasota?

A. Royal Lipizzaner Stallions from Austria.

◆

Q. What Lakeland-born singer and actress appeared in *The Glenn Miller Story* and traveled with Bob Hope to entertain GI's during World War II?

A. Frances Langford.

◆

Q. Pirates of the Caribbean, a Walt Disney World attraction, is situated in what area of the theme park?

A. Adventureland.

◆

Q. What number one hit song did Hank Locklin compose and record in 1958?

A. "Send Me the Pillow That You Dream On."

◆

Q. What Orlando entertainment complex is known for its laughing doors and magic floors?

A. Mystery Fun Houses.

Q. What organization first sponsored the Miss Florida Pageant?

A. The Miami Beach Jaycees.

Q. What member of the hit rock group America was born in Florida in 1950?

A. Dan Peek.

Q. What movie filmed in Pinellas County dealt with the rejuvenation of the elderly by aliens?

A. *Cocoon.*

Q. What aquatic attraction in Florida features monorail rides?

A. Miami Seaquarium.

Q. What award winning actress, born in Pompano Beach, was a regular on the television series "Good Times"?

A. Esther Rolle.

Q. What Fantasyland attraction was first created for the 1964–65 New York's World's Fair?

A. It's a Small World.

Q. Miami Beach is the home of what pop music personality who buys million-dollar mansions and renovates them for resale?

A. Barry Gibb.

Q. Filmed in Dade County, what adventure movie starred Michael Caine as a New York journalist trying to secure a story on a series of yacht disappearances?

A. *The Island.*

———◆———

Q. Disney "AudioAnimatronics" brings to life our nation's chief executives in what patriotic attraction?

A. Hall of Presidents.

———◆———

Q. What Florida-born actor of television and motion pictures appeared in *Chariots of Fire?*

A. Brad Davis.

———◆———

Q. Marianna was the birthplace of what composer/educator who was a pioneer in the field of liturgical jazz?

A. Edgar E. ("Ed") Summerlin.

———◆———

Q. Where can one attend an underwater theater performance of Hans Christian Andersen's *The Little Mermaid?*

A. Weeki Wachee.

———◆———

Q. In what Florida community did Ray Charles live as a small boy?

A. Greenville.

———◆———

Q. Where is the International Worm-Fiddling Contest held?

A. Caryville.

Q. What Jacksonville native was the associate producer of the television series "Rawhide"?

A. A. C. Lyles.

Q. What light-hearted movie starring Hayley Mills was filmed in Hillsborough County in 1986?

A. *Parent Trap II*.

Q. What major attraction in Florida has been dubbed the "thinking man's theme park"?

A. EPCOT Center.

Q. What is the full name of country singer Slim Whitman?

A. Otis Dewey Whitman, Jr.

Q. Where is the Miss Drumstick Pageant held?

A. Spring Hill.

Q. The movie version of Tennessee Williams' *The Rose Tattoo*, starring Burt Lancaster, was filmed in what Florida city?

A. Key West.

Q. What museum in St. Augustine offers exhibits of the odd and unusual from 198 countries?

A. Ripley's Believe It or Not! Museum.

Q. In what Florida community was actress Faye Dunaway born?

A. Bascom.

———◆———

Q. What Jacksonville native was crowned Miss America in 1993?

A. Leansa Cornett.

———◆———

Q. Thelma ("Butterfly") McQueen, best remembered for the role of Prissy in *Gone With the Wind,* was born in 1911 in what city?

A. Tampa.

———◆———

Q. In 1976, what aeronautical adventure movie was shot in Dade County?

A. *Airport '77.*

———◆———

Q. Several original members of what rock band hail from the Jacksonville area?

A. Molly Hatchet.

———◆———

Q. What unusual animal attraction at Pompano Beach features miniature stars of the show?

A. Roger Brown's Miniature Horse Farm.

———◆———

Q. Country singer Bobby Lord was born in what Florida town?

A. Sanford.

Q. What feature movie highlighting strange occurrences off the east coast of Florida was filmed in part of Dade County?

A. *Bermuda Triangle*.

———————◆———————

Q. Where may one ride the Old Town Trolley and the Conch Train?

A. Key West.

———————◆———————

Q. The largest amusement park in the world, Walt Disney World, is situated on how many acres?

A. 27,443.

———————◆———————

Q. What is the name of the ship created by MGM as a movie prop that now is displayed on the St. Petersburg waterfront?

A. The *Bounty*.

———————◆———————

Q. What feature was added to the entertainment at Weeki Wachee Spring in 1947?

A. Live mermaids.

———————◆———————

Q. What Jacksonville-born singer/actor was named one of the Top Ten Recording Artists in 1955 and was selected in 1957 as the third Top Ten Box Office Attraction?

A. Pat Boone.

———————◆———————

Q. A popular entertainment on Key West is to view the spectacular sunsets from what vantage point?

A. Mallory Square Dock in Old Town.

Q. Which James Bond movie, filmed in Marion County in 1982 and starring Sean Connery, begins with Bond being sent to a health farm?

A. *Never Say Never Again.*

Q. What is the name of the marine show and exhibition at Fort Lauderdale?

A. Ocean World.

Q. What famous movie star filmed underwater extravaganzas at Cypress Gardens in the 1950s?

A. Esther Williams.

Q. The intense roller coaster ride in the dark at Walt Disney World is known by what name?

A. Space Mountain.

Q. Miami-born saxophonist Willis Jackson was given what nickname because of a composition he wrote and recorded?

A. "Gator."

Q. Actor Mickey Rourke, who appeared in the movie *Barfly,* was born in 1953 in what city?

A. Miami.

Q. What Floridian southern rock group met its demise in an airplane crash?

A. Lynyrd Skynyrd.

Q. Don Johnson and Philip Michael Thomas acquired instant fame in what popular television series?

A. "Miami Vice."

———◆———

Q. Among the states, where does Florida rank as a film production site?

A. Third (after California and New York).

———◆———

Q. Who composed the 1963 country hit "Detroit City"?

A. Mel Tillis.

———◆———

Q. *Rough Cut,* filmed in Dade County and starring Burt Reynolds, featured what legendary actor in the role of Chief Inspector Cyril Willis?

A. David Niven.

———◆———

Q. What college has the unique Walk of Fame, in which approximately 800 inscribed stones were brought from the homes or birthplaces of famous people?

A. Rollins College, Winter Park.

———◆———

Q. Filmed in Broward County, what 1979 comedy film was set in a research institute run by a small band of insanely mischievous scientists?

A. *Simon.*

———◆———

Q. What Florida attraction once offered a person the opportunity to take a 20th Century-Fox screen test?

A. The Stars Hall of Fame, Orlando.

Q. In what city did pop star Jimmy Buffett pen many of his early ballads?

A. Key West.

◆

Q. What Quincy-born jazz musician composed the movie score for *The Honey Baby*?

A. Nathaniel ("Nat") Adderley, Jr.

◆

Q. What movie based on the Tom Wolfe novel of the same name follows the development of the space program?

A. *The Right Stuff.*

◆

Q. What Miami-born musician was Dinah Shore's drummer from 1967 to 1970?

A. David A. ("Panama") Francis.

◆

Q. What MGM movie starring Floridian actress Faye Dunaway was shot in Dade County in 1978?

A. *The Champ.*

◆

Q. What star of stage, screen, and television was born in Ocala in 1941?

A. Elizabeth Ashley.

◆

Q. Kissimmee is the host for what category of music festival each spring?

A. Bluegrass.

Q. What 1977 television movie was shot in Sarasota County, depicting the lives of one of the all-time great circus families?

A. *The Great Wallendas.*

Q. What attraction at the junction of U.S. 27 and I–4 features the world of the Big Top?

A. Circus World.

Q. On what Fort Lauderdale vessel may people take a three-hour cruise on the Intercoastal Waterway?

A. The Paddlewheel Queen.

Q. Sam Jones, bass player who toured with C. Adderley, D. Gillespie, and T. Monk, was from what Florida city?

A. Jacksonville.

Q. What rock musician, born December 8, 1943, in Melbourne, helped form The Doors?

A. James Douglas (Jim Morrison).

Q. What 1980 science fiction motion picture starring Kirk Douglas as Capt. Matthew Yelland was filmed in part in Monroe County?

A. *The Final Countdown.*

Q. In what movie was Captain Tony's Saloon in Key West used as a set?

A. *Kill Castro.*

Q. What made-for-television movie shot in Monroe County in 1979 dealt with the life and times of Dr. Samuel Mudd?

A. *The Ordeal of Dr. Mudd.*

———◆———

Q. What city hosted the Miss Florida Pageant from 1949 to 1953?

A. Jacksonville.

———◆———

Q. What 1981 action movie, filmed in part in Dade County, starred Christopher Walken as the leader of a group of mercenaries who staged a coup in a small West African country?

A. *The Dogs of War.*

———◆———

Q. Where is the Miss Firecracker contest held?

A. Tampa.

———◆———

Q. What Florida-born country music singer recorded such hits as "North Wind," "Secret Love," and "Indian Love Call"?

A. Slim Whitman.

———◆———

Q. In 1970, what Tampa native edited the *Motion Picture Almanac* and the *TV Almanac*?

A. Richard Gertner.

———◆———

Q. What Floridian actress played Bonnie in the 1967 box office hit *Bonnie and Clyde*?

A. Faye Dunaway.

Q. What Miami-born director/producer has the *Naked Zoo* and *Live and Let Die* to his credits?

A. William Grefe.

———◆———

Q. Which is America's southernmost championship rodeo?

A. The Homestead Rodeo.

———◆———

Q. What Miami native played trumpet for Ray Charles from 1969 to 1971?

A. Richard Allen ("Blue") Mitchell.

———◆———

Q. What 1983 Disney Production, featuring a mermaid as the main character, was shot in Dade County?

A. *Splash.*

———◆———

Q. What Pensacola-born tenor sax jazz musician has worked with such groups as Horace Silver, Blue Mitchell, and the George Coleman Octet?

A. Herman ("Junior") Cook.

———◆———

Q. Paramount Pictures filmed what television pilot in Monroe County in 1978?

A. "Divers of the Coral Reef."

———◆———

Q. What famous country singer, known as the "First Lady of Country Music," maintains a home in Jupiter?

A. Tammy Wynette.

Q. What 1977 film shot in Dade County featured Burt Reynolds and Kris Kristofferson as two football players involved in a romantic triangle with the team owner's daughter, Jill Clayburgh?

A. *Semi-Tough.*

Q. What Miami-born drummer toured with Nancy Wilson, Duke Pearson's Big Band, and Dizzy Gillespie?

A. Granville William ("Mickey") Roker.

Q. What 1984 horror feature was filmed in Lee County?

A. *Day of the Dead.*

Q. What jazz festival is held along the St. Johns River?

A. Mayport and All That Jazz.

Q. What 1979 PBS special was filmed in Pinellas County?

A. "The Golden Honeymoon."

Q. Where was the classic science fiction movie *The Creature from the Black Lagoon* shot?

A. Wakulla Springs.

Q. What noted saxophonist/composer, born in Tampa, served on the jazz advisory panel for the Kennedy Performing Arts Center?

A. Julian Edwin ("Cannonball") Adderley.

HISTORY

Q. What was the name of the first manned moon mission that lifted off from Kennedy Space Center on July 16, 1969?

A. Apollo 11.

———◆———

Q. Florida began using what form of capital punishment in 1924?

A. The electric chair.

———◆———

Q. What was the largest city in Florida in 1890?

A. Key West, population 18,000.

———◆———

Q. Where was a so-called "colony for feeble-minded children" established in 1921?

A. Gainesville.

———◆———

Q. Where was the first official news of the sinking of the USS *Maine* in Havana harbor received on February 15, 1898?

A. The International Ocean Telegraph Company office at Punta Rassa.

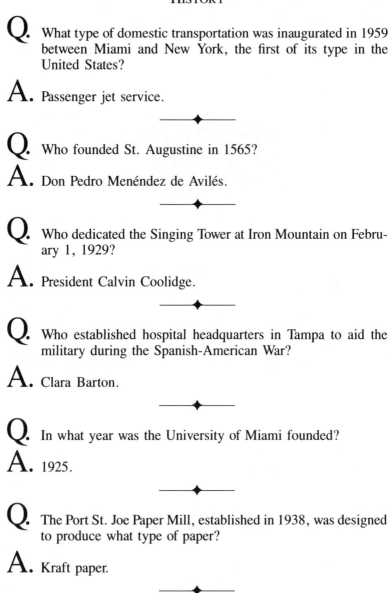

Q. What type of domestic transportation was inaugurated in 1959 between Miami and New York, the first of its type in the United States?

A. Passenger jet service.

Q. Who founded St. Augustine in 1565?

A. Don Pedro Menéndez de Avilés.

Q. Who dedicated the Singing Tower at Iron Mountain on February 1, 1929?

A. President Calvin Coolidge.

Q. Who established hospital headquarters in Tampa to aid the military during the Spanish-American War?

A. Clara Barton.

Q. In what year was the University of Miami founded?

A. 1925.

Q. The Port St. Joe Paper Mill, established in 1938, was designed to produce what type of paper?

A. Kraft paper.

Q. What caused one span of the Sunshine Skyway Bridge to collapse on May 9, 1980, taking the lives of thirty-five motorists?

A. A freighter collision.

Q. What junior college was established in Sarasota in 1931?

A. Ringling Junior College.

———◆———

Q. What labor law was passed in Florida in 1935?

A. Workers' Compensation.

———◆———

Q. Who was the Communist candidate for president who was attacked at a political rally in Tampa in 1936?

A. Earl Browder.

———◆———

Q. What great economic boom in Florida went bust in 1926?

A. Real estate.

———◆———

Q. By 1860, what crop had become the economic basis of Florida?

A. Cotton.

———◆———

Q. During the 1850s and 1860s, what steamboat company became the principal operator on the St. Johns River?

A. The Brock Line.

———◆———

Q. The Labor Day hurricane of 1935 destroyed how many miles of overseas railroad in the Florida Keys?

A. Thirty-eight.

Q. What state-sponsored school was opened in St. Augustine in 1883?

A. Florida State School for the Deaf and Blind.

Q. What federal agency began operations at Cape Canaveral in 1958?

A. National Aeronautics and Space Administration (NASA).

Q. What U.S. highway was extended down abandoned railroad causeways in the keys in 1937 and 1938, creating an unbroken road from Maine to Key West?

A. U.S. 1.

Q. The Florida legislature enacted a law in 1937 that allowed railroad companies to operate what type of equipment in connection with their rail service?

A. Trucks for pick-up, delivery, and short hauls.

Q. Who was the first black admitted to the Florida bar?

A. Poet James Weldon Johnson (1871–1938).

Q. What was Gen. Joseph Warren Stilwell's nickname during World War II?

A. "Vinegar Joe."

Q. Who paid five hundred dollars at an auction for the first passenger ticket on the maiden flight of Florida's first airline?

A. A. C. Pheil, mayor of St. Petersburg.

Q. At the time of the Spanish conquest of Florida, what four Indian tribes dominated the region?

A. Calusa, Tegesta, Timucuan, and Apalachee.

———◆———

Q. In 1938, what streamlined passenger train, pulled by the world's largest and most powerful diesel-electric locomotives, was placed in service between New York and Miami?

A. *The Silver Meteor.*

———◆———

Q. How many Floridians served in the Confederate army?

A. Approximately 15,000.

———◆———

Q. What governor died on September 28, 1953, during his first year of office?

A. Dan T. McCarty.

———◆———

Q. Who first planted avocados in Florida in 1833?

A. Henry Perrine.

———◆———

Q. In 1956, who became the first gubernatorial candidate to win a first-primary victory?

A. LeRoy Collins.

———◆———

Q. What was the name of the plantation of John Moultrie, who served as the lieutenant governor under English rule from 1763 to 1783?

A. Belle Vista.

Q. On what date did Florida gain statehood?

A. March 3, 1845.

———◆———

Q. Under the Corrupt Practices Law of 1913, what was the maximum one could spend in Florida while seeking the governorship or a U.S. Senate seat?

A. Four thousand dollars.

———◆———

Q. In 1949, the legislature passed laws banning what from highways?

A. Livestock.

———◆———

Q. What was the first southern college to present an honorary degree to a black woman?

A. Rollins College, Winter Park, to Mary McLeod Bethune.

———◆———

Q. What community had to call out the Home Guard in 1918 to protect the local bank, because of the large deposits made from the sale of potatoes to buyers from potato-scarce northern markets?

A. Hastings.

———◆———

Q. What was the slogan of the Florida Forest Service Nursery when it was founded in Raiford in 1920?

A. "Plant Idle Acres."

———◆———

Q. Which American Revolutionary War general, along with his 3,000 soldiers, was repulsed in his invasion of Florida in 1778 by 1,210 British soldiers, Florida woodsmen, and Indians?

A. Gen. Robert Howe.

Q. Who first discovered phosphate deposits on the Peace River in 1884?

A. J. Francis LeBaron.

———◆———

Q. Approximately how many U.S. soldiers died in the Seminole Wars?

A. Fifteen hundred.

———◆———

Q. Built between 1851 and 1865, the massive brick structure of Fort Jefferson was known by what nickname?

A. "The Gibraltar of the Gulf of Mexico."

———◆———

Q. What was the construction cost of the Tamiami Trail highway?

A. Thirteen million dollars.

———◆———

Q. What Palatka-born U.S. general was the first American to command a Chinese army?

A. Joseph Warren Stilwell.

———◆———

Q. Where was the first public school established in Florida in 1852?

A. Tallahassee.

———◆———

Q. By what name did the federal government refer to Chief Billy Bowlegs?

A. Mr. William B. Legs.

Q. Whose architectural designs were utilized in the late 1930s at Florida Southern College?

A. Frank Lloyd Wright.

Q. Who became known as the "father of Florida cooperative marketing" in the late 1800s?

A. Dr. F. W. Inman.

Q. Near what town, on the northern edge of Lake Weir, were "Ma" ("Machine-Gun Kate") Barker and her son, Fred, killed in a gun battle with federal agents on January 16, 1935?

A. Ocklawaha.

Q. During Spanish rule, what was the name of the outpost of St. Augustine that was manned by escaped slaves from the Carolinas?

A. Fort Moosa.

Q. When Henry Flagler built his seventy-three-room Palm Beach mansion in 1901, he gave it what name?

A. Whitehall.

Q. The prehistoric Indians of northern Florida began manufacturing what type of utensils around 2,000 B.C.?

A. Ceramic pottery.

Q. Approximately how many people were drowned by the hurricane-driven waters of Lake Okeechokee in 1928?

A. Fifteen hundred.

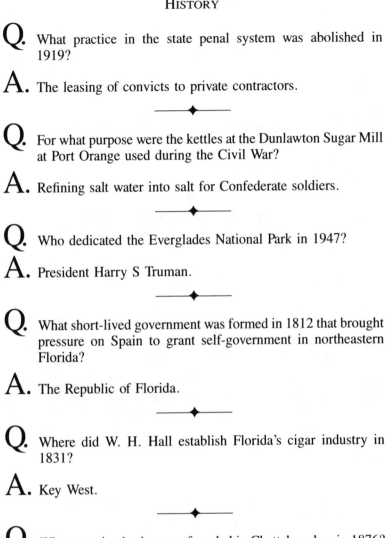

Q. What practice in the state penal system was abolished in 1919?

A. The leasing of convicts to private contractors.

------◆------

Q. For what purpose were the kettles at the Dunlawton Sugar Mill at Port Orange used during the Civil War?

A. Refining salt water into salt for Confederate soldiers.

------◆------

Q. Who dedicated the Everglades National Park in 1947?

A. President Harry S Truman.

------◆------

Q. What short-lived government was formed in 1812 that brought pressure on Spain to grant self-government in northeastern Florida?

A. The Republic of Florida.

------◆------

Q. Where did W. H. Hall establish Florida's cigar industry in 1831?

A. Key West.

------◆------

Q. What state institution was founded in Chattahoochee in 1876?

A. The Florida State Hospital for the Insane.

------◆------

Q. Inaugurated on January 1, 1914, what was the world's first scheduled commercial airline?

A. The St. Petersburg-Tampa Airboat Line.

Q. Who bought a house in Ft. Myers adjacent to the grounds of Thomas A. Edison's home?

A. Henry Ford.

———◆———

Q. What noted voodoo doctor lived and practiced in Lawtey in the 1920s and 1930s?

A. Dr. H. W. Abraham.

———◆———

Q. In 1914, what military installation was established in the Panhandle with six airplanes, nine officers, and twenty-three enlisted men?

A. The Pensacola Naval Air Station.

———◆———

Q. The Civil War cost Florida about how many lives?

A. Approximately five thousand.

———◆———

Q. In the early Spanish mission towns established among the Indians, who was the only Spaniard allowed to be a permanent resident?

A. The priest.

———◆———

Q. At what percentage did the unemployment rate in Florida peak in 1975?

A. Thirteen percent.

———◆———

Q. What building was admired by William Randolph Hearst on a trip to Spain and then purchased, dismantled, and shipped to Miami, where it was reassembled?

A. The Cloisters of the Monastery of St. Bernard de Clairvaux, originally built in 1141.

Q. Where was the Florida Baptist Children's Home established in 1907?

A. Arcadia.

———◆———

Q. What type of weapons were denied by the Spanish government to the Indians who lived in the early mission towns?

A. Firearms of any type.

———◆———

Q. During the Civil War, what did Mrs. Sarah Orman of Apalachicola use to signal Confederate troops as to the presence of Federal troops in town?

A. A large wooden keg on her roof.

———◆———

Q. Who was the pilot of Florida's first airline?

A. Tony Jannus.

———◆———

Q. The State Board of Health was created in 1889 to fight what disease?

A. Yellow fever.

———◆———

Q. What name was given to the mass exodus of some 125,000 refugees from Cuba to Florida in 1980?

A. The Freedom Flotilla.

———◆———

Q. Who was the political and labor activist who was kidnapped and beaten to death in Tampa in 1935?

A. Joseph Shoemaker.

HISTORY

Q. Who was the internationally known south Florida banker who was a close acquaintance of Richard M. Nixon?

A. Charles ("Bebe") Rebozo.

Q. According to census figures, how many slaves were held in northern Florida in 1860?

A. 61,475.

Q. Who was the notorious fugitive wanted for several killings in Georgia and in the Key West area who lived for many years around Chokoloskee until he was killed by a local posse?

A. Ed ("Emperor") Watson.

Q. Highway U.S. 41, completed in 1928 and connecting Miami with the Gulf coast via the Everglades, also is known by what name?

A. The Tamiami Trail.

Q. In 1834, what railroad line became the first to be chartered in Florida?

A. The Tallahassee Railroad Company.

Q. What prerequisite to voting was abolished in 1937?

A. The state poll tax.

Q. What was the name of the unsuccessful organization formed in Tallahassee in 1831 to further education in Florida?

A. Florida Educational Society.

Q. Where did John J. Pershing, a lieutenant serving as quartermaster to the all-black Tenth Cavalry, receive his nickname, "Black Jack," in 1898?

A. Lakeland.

———◆———

Q. What two steamers, placed in service in 1886, provided the first through service by water between Jacksonville and New York City?

A. The SS *Cherokee* and SS *Seminole*.

———◆———

Q. What unusual canning facility was established in Arcadia in 1931 and relocated near Port Tampa City in 1937?

A. End's Rattlesnake Cannery and Reptilorium.

———◆———

Q. What two forms of punishment for convicts were abolished in the state penal system in 1923?

A. The lash and the sweatbox.

———◆———

Q. In 1924, the *Apache* became the first passenger steamship to provide service between New York and what Florida city?

A. Miami.

———◆———

Q. How many people were killed in the hurricane of 1928?

A. 1,810.

———◆———

Q. What fortification built by the Spanish at Pensacola in 1698 was destroyed by the French in 1719?

A. Fort San Carlos.

Q. Chronologically, where did Florida rank in order of states seceding from the Union?

A. Third.

◆

Q. The lavish Italian Renaissance-style villa of industrialist James Deering was completed in 1920 on Biscayne Bay at what cost?

A. Fifteen million dollars.

◆

Q. Between 1848 and 1857, where were 499 ocean vessels destroyed?

A. The Florida Reef.

◆

Q. Where did the sponge industry relocate when new, extensive sponge beds were discovered in 1905?

A. Tarpon Springs.

◆

Q. In what year did the state begin draining the Everglades to form agricultural land?

A. 1906.

◆

Q. What Alabama businessman bought Key West in 1821 for two thousand dollars?

A. John Simonton.

◆

Q. A statue of what Tallahassee-born Confederate general represents Florida in the U.S. Capitol?

A. Edmund Kirby Smith.

Q. What Latvian immigrant created Coral Castle, north of Homestead, from 1925 to 1940?

A. Edward Leedskalnin.

Q. What board was established in 1935 to regulate the citrus industry?

A. The Florida Citrus Commission.

Q. During World War II, what famous general, along with his flight crews, received special training at Eglin Air Force Base prior to their April 1942 air raid on Tokyo, Japan?

A. Gen. Jimmy Doolittle.

Q. Which Seminole leader surrendered with his warriors in 1858, ending the third Seminole conflict?

A. Chief Billy Bowlegs.

Q. In 1966, who became Florida's first Republican governor since 1877?

A. Claude R. Kirk, Jr. (1967–71).

Q. What three astronauts were killed at Cape Kennedy in 1967 by a fire aboard Apollo I?

A. Virgil I. Grissom, Edward H. White, and Roger B. Chaffee.

Q. For what communication system was a state regulatory authority established in Florida in 1911?

A. Telephone.

Q. Who was the thirty-two-year-old doctor who set the broken leg of assassin John Wilkes Booth and was imprisoned on the Dry Tortugas in 1865 on conspiracy charges?

A. Dr. Samuel A. Mudd.

◆

Q. What educational board was established by the legislature in 1955?

A. The Community College Council.

◆

Q. What venom laboratory began operation in Miami in 1948?

A. Miami Serpentarium.

◆

Q. What "hurricane-proof" hostelry was built at Fort Lauderdale in 1905?

A. The New River Inn.

◆

Q. What was the name of the 1767 road connecting New Smyrna, St. Augustine, and the border of Georgia?

A. The King's Road.

◆

Q. In 1886, the city council of De Land passed what type of incentive to property owners who would plant trees of two or more inches in diameter along the city's streets?

A. A fifty-cent tax rebate per tree.

◆

Q. What railroad line in 1912 connected Key West and the Florida Keys to the rest of the state by constructing overseas bridges?

A. Florida East Coast Railway.

Q. Who set an all-time national record by receiving a doctorate at the age of ninety-two from Florida State University?

A. Virgil Conner.

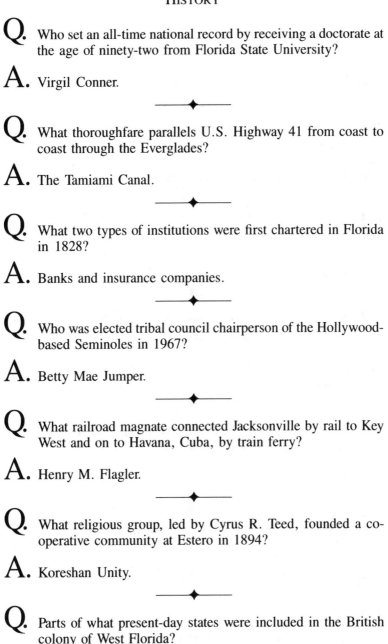

Q. What thoroughfare parallels U.S. Highway 41 from coast to coast through the Everglades?

A. The Tamiami Canal.

Q. What two types of institutions were first chartered in Florida in 1828?

A. Banks and insurance companies.

Q. Who was elected tribal council chairperson of the Hollywood-based Seminoles in 1967?

A. Betty Mae Jumper.

Q. What railroad magnate connected Jacksonville by rail to Key West and on to Havana, Cuba, by train ferry?

A. Henry M. Flagler.

Q. What religious group, led by Cyrus R. Teed, founded a co-operative community at Estero in 1894?

A. Koreshan Unity.

Q. Parts of what present-day states were included in the British colony of West Florida?

A. Florida, Alabama, Mississippi, and Louisiana.

Q. Who was the first recorded black to visit Florida, a slave with the Narváez Expedition in 1528?

A. Estevanico.

———◆———

Q. In 1702, what Englishman laid siege to St. Augustine for three months?

A. James Moore, governor of the Council of South Carolina.

———◆———

Q. Where was the State Agricultural College situated from 1883 to 1905?

A. Lake City.

———◆———

Q. What Miami woman grabbed the would-be assassin's arm, thus deflecting the bullet and saving the life of Franklin Roosevelt in 1933?

A. Lillian Cross.

———◆———

Q. In 1943, a tax was placed on what luxury item to help replace horse and dog racing revenues lost during the war?

A. Cigarettes.

———◆———

Q. How many times has Miami Beach hosted a national political convention?

A. Three (Democratic, 1972; Republican, 1968, 1972).

———◆———

Q. What military garrison was established in 1839 and named for the then chief quartermaster of Florida?

A. Fort Myers.

Q. A monument to what ill-fated invasion of Cuba is situated in the Cuban Memorial Plaza in Miami?

A. The Bay of Pigs.

———◆———

Q. What railroad line was constructed by Henry B. Plant between Kissimmee and Tampa in 1883–84 in less than seven months?

A. The South Florida Railroad.

———◆———

Q. Following the Civil War, when was Florida readmitted to the Union?

A. June 25, 1868.

———◆———

Q. Which presidential candidate carried 51.93 percent of Florida's general election vote in 1976?

A. Jimmy Carter.

———◆———

Q. What price was paid in 1819 for the area of De Leon Springs, then known as Spring Garden?

A. Fifty black women.

———◆———

Q. Who was the British royalty, cousin of Queen Victoria, who deserted his family in England and relocated in the Tarpon Springs area in 1886 with a lady friend?

A. The Duke of Sutherland.

———◆———

Q. How many students were enrolled in the University of Florida at Gainesville for its opening semester in 1906?

A. Fewer than 100.

Q. What airline in the 1930s established the world's largest commercial marine air base in Miami?

A. Pan American.

———◆———

Q. Was Florida admitted to the Union as a free or a slave state?

A. A slave state.

———◆———

Q. What plantation was established near Capps in 1828 by Virginia planter John Nuttall and his sons, James and William B.?

A. El Destino Plantation.

———◆———

Q. In 1860, the Florida Railroad connected what two towns, thereby forming the first cross-state line?

A. Fernandina and Cedar Key.

———◆———

Q. What industry was first opened at Key West in 1849?

A. The sponge industry.

———◆———

Q. When was the Ordinance of Secession passed, severing Florida's ties with the Union?

A. January 10, 1861.

———◆———

Q. Five thousand Floridians volunteered to fight in what war?

A. The Spanish-American War.

Q. For what amount—not a cent of which was actually ever paid—did Spain sell Florida to the United States on February 22, 1819?

A. Five million dollars.

———◆———

Q. In 1946, what president chose Key West for his "Little White House"?

A. Harry S Truman.

———◆———

Q. The passage of the Social Welfare Act by the Florida legislature in 1935 led to the establishment of what department?

A. The State Welfare Board.

———◆———

Q. In 1934, a truce signed between what two parties was publicized as bringing to an end the longest war in the nation's history?

A. The Seminole Indians and the U.S. government.

———◆———

Q. In what state was Thomas Edison's Fort Myers home originally built?

A. Maine.

———◆———

Q. What lottery operated at Port Tampa City from 1893 until it was closed by the federal government in 1895?

A. The Honduras National Lottery.

———◆———

Q. Where was Confederate general Stonewall Jackson stationed in 1851?

A. Fort Meade.

Q. For what purpose were 140 oak logs recovered in 1926 from a pond on the Pensacola Naval Air Station grounds, where they had rested since the Civil War, and shipped to the Boston Navy Yard?

A. For restoration work on the USS *Constitution*.

———◆———

Q. In its peak days as a port town, how many foreign consuls were based at Fernandina?

A. Fourteen.

———◆———

Q. What general commanded the Confederate troops at the Battle of Olustee?

A. Gen. Joseph Finnegan.

———◆———

Q. What great Apache chief, along with his followers, was imprisoned at Fort Pickens in Pensacola Harbor in 1886?

A. Geronimo.

———◆———

Q. From what source did the community of Bagdad receive its name in the early 1850s?

A. The Bagdad Lumber Company.

———◆———

Q. What epidemic killed three-fourths of the residents of St. Joseph in 1841 and caused the remainder to abandon the town?

A. Yellow fever, brought by ship from South America.

———◆———

Q. What was the name of the Miami home, constructed in 1915, of the noted orator and politician William Jennings Bryan?

A. Villa Serena.

Q. What state bureau was established in 1868?

A. The Bureau of Immigration.

———◆———

Q. What 1970 event in Tampa Bay brought the issue of the area's ecology into sharp focus?

A. A major oil spill.

———◆———

Q. What human institution has been recorded in Florida state records since 1927?

A. Marriages.

———◆———

Q. On May 5, 1961, who was the first astronaut to be launched on a suborbital flight from Cape Canaveral?

A. Navy Comdr. Alan Shepard.

———◆———

Q. Mary M. Bethune, president of Bethune-Cookman College in Daytona Beach until 1942, attained what prestigious governmental honor?

A. She was the first black woman to head a federal agency, the Division of Negro Affairs, National Youth Administration.

———◆———

Q. The state legislature authorized what transportation system in 1955?

A. The Florida Turnpike.

———◆———

Q. What trend-setting marine attraction opened south of St. Augustine in 1938?

A. Marineland of Florida.

Q. What university held its first classes at Boca Raton in 1964?

A. Florida Atlantic University.

———◆———

Q. What change was made in 1963 in the election system of the governor and cabinet?

A. They were moved to nonpresidential years.

———◆———

Q. What new source of revenue was legalized in 1931?

A. Pari-mutuel betting on dog and horse races.

———◆———

Q. What notorious band of desperadoes was gunned down in 1924 at the Sebastian River Bridge near the community of Micco?

A. The Ashley Gang.

———◆———

Q. What Pensacola-born woman organized and commanded the Women Airforce Service Pilots (WASPs) during World War II?

A. Jacqueline Cochran.

———◆———

Q. An English buccaneer named Davis sacked what Spanish town in 1668?

A. St. Augustine.

———◆———

Q. What Florida city had the highest murder rate in the nation in 1980?

A. Miami.

Q. Following the panic of 1837, the Florida constitution was amended to make it unlawful for the state to go into debt and for what type of business people to hold public office?

A. Bankers.

————◆————

Q. On May 13, 1973, what U.S. space station was launched from Kennedy Space Center?

A. Skylab.

————◆————

Q. What coastal city did Gen. Andrew Jackson and his troops seize in 1814?

A. Pensacola.

————◆————

Q. In 1963, who changed the name of Cape Canaveral to Cape Kennedy and the NASA installation to the John F. Kennedy Space Center?

A. Jackie Kennedy persuaded President Lyndon Johnson to ask the governor of Florida to change the name.

————◆————

Q. Who became Florida's first black secretary of state in 1869?

A. Jonathan C. Gibbs.

————◆————

Q. What company was authorized in 1879 to construct a canal between Lake Eustis and Lake Apopka?

A. The Apopka Canal Company.

————◆————

Q. By 1840, what town had become the third largest port on the Gulf of Mexico for the shipment of cotton?

A. Apalachicola.

Q. What was the name of America's first earth satellite, launched from Cape Canaveral in 1958?

A. Explorer I.

Q. Who was the Fort Lauderdale building contractor who first developed the hollow concrete block?

A. Edwin Thomas King.

Q. What was the official name of the Yulee railroad?

A. The Atlantic, Gulf, and West Indies Transit Company.

Q. What piece of legislation brought about sweeping reform in the state's educational system in 1905?

A. The Buckman Act.

Q. Who operated the first schools in Florida during the 1600s?

A. Spanish priests.

Q. The bulk of what industry relocated to Tampa in 1886, after its factories burned to the ground in Key West?

A. The cigar industry.

Q. When established in 1865, what amount did Florida's Civil War pension plan pay to women widowed by the war?

A. Eight dollars every three months.

Q. The first airline in Florida operated for how long?

A. Twenty-eight consecutive days.

———◆———

Q. What white carpenter was branded and jailed in the 1840s after being found guilty by a Pensacola court of abducting slaves?

A. Jonathan Walker.

———◆———

Q. On May 30, 1539, what famous Spanish explorer, along with 700 soldiers, landed in the Tampa area?

A. Hernando de Soto.

———◆———

Q. Who was the citrus promotion spokesperson of the late 1970s who received national attention for her views about equal rights laws for homosexuals?

A. Anita Bryant.

———◆———

Q. In 1919, Florida began to keep registration records on what natural human event?

A. Deaths.

———◆———

Q. At which battle did cadets from West Florida Seminary and members of the Home Guard turn back Union forces from capturing Tallahassee in 1865?

A. The Battle of Natural Bridge.

———◆———

Q. What city was first in the nation to create a metropolitan (Metro) government, combining city and county functions?

A. Miami (1957).

Q. Who became the first territorial governor of Florida in the spring of 1822?

A. William P. DuVal.

------◆------

Q. Hurricane Cleo cost how much in property damage in 1964?

A. More than $115 million.

------◆------

Q. How did William Marvin become governor of Florida in 1865?

A. President Andrew Johnson appointed him.

------◆------

Q. The Hillsborough Lighthouse, completed in 1907, boasted a light of how much strength?

A. 5.5 million candlepower.

------◆------

Q. Where, on February 20, 1864, was the biggest battle in Florida of the Civil War fought?

A. Near Olustee.

------◆------

Q. Who was the leader of refugee blacks who allied with the Seminole Indian chief Osceola against government troops in the 1830s?

A. Ino.

------◆------

Q. What type of furnishings, installed in downtown St. Petersburg in 1907, have become something of a trademark?

A. Green benches.

Q. What Miami Baptist pastor personally assisted in the immigration and relocation of several thousand Cuban refugees in the early 1960s?

A. The Rev. Daniel G. Rodriguez.

Q. To what position was Gen. Andrew Jackson appointed in Florida during July 1821?

A. Military commander.

Q. What state law enforcement agency was established in 1939?

A. The Florida Highway Patrol.

Q. What noted Union general in the Civil War was stationed as a lieutenant at Fort Peyton near Moultrie during the latter part of the Seminole Wars?

A. William Tecumseh Sherman.

Q. Construction began on what major dam within the state in 1949?

A. The Jim Woodruff Dam.

Q. In 1783, England ceded Florida holdings back to what country?

A. Spain.

Q. Florida has favored which political party for most of its history?

A. Democratic.

Q. What percentage of Florida's population in 1900 was black?

A. Forty-five percent.

◆

Q. Who from Orlando became the first person to solo in a balloon across the Atlantic Ocean in September 1984?

A. Joe Kittinger.

◆

Q. Who was the buccaneering adventurer who incited the Indians against both American and Spanish settlements during the first decade of the nineteenth century?

A. William Bowles.

◆

Q. What is the statewide sales tax in Florida?

A. Six percent.

◆

Q. What noted orthopedic surgeon, who was a consultant for the Byrd Antarctic Expedition, founded the Florida Medical Center at Venice in 1935?

A. Dr. Joseph Braden.

◆

Q. For whom was the Florida Key Tavernier named?

A. A French pirate of the 1800s.

◆

Q. What monetary figure has been placed on the costs and damages of the Seminole Wars?

A. $40 million.

Q. Who built Florida's first modern swimming pool in 1900?

A. Thomas A. Edison.

———◆———

Q. Who deceived and captured Osceola while under a flag of truce in 1837?

A. Gen. Thomas S. Jessup.

———◆———

Q. Due to state legislation, what Tallahassee institution was transferred to the status of a coeducational college for blacks?

A. Florida Agricultural and Mechanical College.

———◆———

Q. Where were fifty-five eight-passenger canoes built and placed in service during the Seminole Wars?

A. Fort Ogden.

———◆———

Q. What settlement had the largest number of British sponsored colonists in the New World in 1767?

A. New Smyrna.

———◆———

Q. What U.S. senator from Florida resigned his position to become secretary of the Confederate navy?

A. Stephen Russell Mallory.

———◆———

Q. Where was the Peace Memorial Church constructed in 1923 in honor of those killed in World War I?

A. Clearwater.

Q. The Palm Beach mansion Mar-a-Largo was owned by what prominent heiress?

A. Marjorie Merriweather Post, of cereal fame.

———◆———

Q. Where in 1930 did John D. Rockefeller take his first airplane ride, although the plane never left the ground?

A. Ormond Beach.

———◆———

Q. What motto was inscribed on the hats of the school-age Confederate soldiers known as the "Baby Corps"?

A. "To Tallahassee or Hell."

———◆———

Q. Near what present-day community were Maj. Francis L. Dade and 108 of his 109 men killed in a Seminole Indian attack?

A. Bushnell.

———◆———

Q. Funding for what kind of new educational endeavor was authorized in 1957?

A. Educational television.

———◆———

Q. Latin-Americans in the cigar industry formed what organization in the early 1880s?

A. The first union in Florida.

———◆———

Q. In 1763, Spain gave Florida to England in exchange for what land?

A. Cuba.

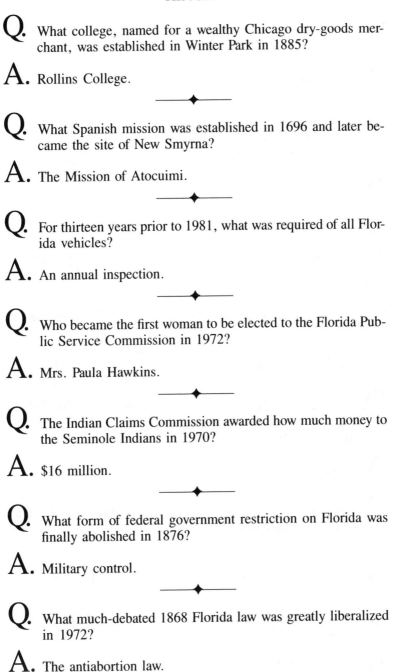

Q. What college, named for a wealthy Chicago dry-goods merchant, was established in Winter Park in 1885?

A. Rollins College.

Q. What Spanish mission was established in 1696 and later became the site of New Smyrna?

A. The Mission of Atocuimi.

Q. For thirteen years prior to 1981, what was required of all Florida vehicles?

A. An annual inspection.

Q. Who became the first woman to be elected to the Florida Public Service Commission in 1972?

A. Mrs. Paula Hawkins.

Q. The Indian Claims Commission awarded how much money to the Seminole Indians in 1970?

A. $16 million.

Q. What form of federal government restriction on Florida was finally abolished in 1876?

A. Military control.

Q. What much-debated 1868 Florida law was greatly liberalized in 1972?

A. The antiabortion law.

Q. In February 1933, who attempted to assassinate president-elect Franklin D. Roosevelt in Miami?

A. Guiseppe Zangara.

Q. What politically oriented Cuban fraternal order was prevalent in Key West and Tampa during the later part of the nineteenth century and the early part of the twentieth century?

A. The Nanigo.

Q. To what was the drinking age raised in 1980?

A. Nineteen, with the exclusion of military personnel, who continued to be able to drink at age eighteen.

Q. Where was the nation's second civic center established in 1885?

A. De Funiak Springs.

Q. In 1979, what former Florida Power Corporation Board chairman was given a six-month sentence for his involvement in the "daisychain" oil scandal?

A. Angel P. Perez.

Q. What two great Spanish treasure ships, which sank in 1622, have been located by Mel Fisher and his Treasure Salvors, Inc.?

A. The *Nuestra Senora de Atocha* and *Santa Margarita*.

Q. What Democratic presidential candidate carried Florida in the 1904 election?

A. Alton B. Parker (his opponent, Theodore Roosevelt, won).

Q. What wrecked slave ship escapee became a lieutenant of the notorious pirate Blackbeard?

A. Black Caesar.

———————◆———————

Q. Who was elected mayor of Moore Haven in 1917, thus becoming one of the first women in the nation to hold that office?

A. Mrs. J. J. O'Brien.

———————◆———————

Q. What secret organization was formed by Thomas W. Oskorne in 1867 to help secure the participation of blacks in state politics?

A. The Lincoln Brotherhood.

———————◆———————

Q. Who laid out plans between 1915 and 1920 for Florida's first extensive highway system?

A. Michael McKenzie Smith.

———————◆———————

Q. What Tampa physician established a mutual benefit society for medical care in the 1880s?

A. Dr. Guillermo Machado.

———————◆———————

Q. At the time of his death in 1939, who was the largest land-owner in Florida?

A. Barron G. Collier.

———————◆———————

Q. Where did the first constitutional convention of Florida convene on February 1, 1838?

A. St. Joseph.

Q. What spiritualist founded Camp Cassadaga near Orange City in 1893 for meetings of the Cassadaga Spiritualist Association?

A. George B. Colby.

———◆———

Q. What was the name of John D. Rockefeller's winter home in Ormond Beach?

A. The Casements.

———◆———

Q. What trans-state highway was opened in the southern part of the state on April 25, 1928?

A. The Tamiami Trail.

———◆———

Q. What longtime U.S. senator and congressman served as chair of the House Select Committee on Aging?

A. Claude Pepper.

———◆———

Q. In what community did a race riot on November 3, 1920, leave two whites and thirty-five blacks dead?

A. Ocoee.

———◆———

Q. What lighthouse, built in 1860, still guides ships with a beam visible eighteen miles at sea?

A. Jupiter Lighthouse.

———◆———

Q. Into what type of geopolitical entity was Florida formed on March 3, 1821?

A. It became a territory of the United States.

ARTS & LITERATURE

C H A P T E R F O U R

Q. What young English journalist reported developments of the Spanish-American War in Cuba while he lived in Tampa?

A. Winston Churchill.

Q. Where did Sen. John F. Kennedy write his best seller, *Profiles in Courage*?

A. Palm Beach.

Q. What song was recorded on the world's first record, now on display at the Edison Museum in Fort Myers?

A. "Mary Had a Little Lamb."

Q. The world's largest collection of art by what famous Spanish surrealist is on display in St. Petersburg?

A. Salvador Dali.

Q. What two Key West bars were favorites of novelist Ernest Hemingway?

A. Sloppy Joe's and Captain Tony's Saloon.

Q. Shirley Christian received a 1981 Pulitzer Prize for international reporting while associated with what Florida newspaper?

A. *Miami Herald.*

◆

Q. What became the official state play in 1973?

A. *Cross and Sword.*

◆

Q. What is the name of the Florida Philharmonic's series of pop concerts?

A. Pops by the Bay (Fort Lauderdale).

◆

Q. The building housing the Pensacola Art Center was formerly used for what purpose?

A. A jail.

◆

Q. Lake Placid is host to what competition for amateur and professional craftsmen?

A. Arts & Crafts Country Fair.

◆

Q. What architect designed many Spanish-Mediterranean buildings and mansions seen today in Palm Beach?

A. Addison Mizner.

◆

Q. What Fort Myers resident owns the world's largest collection of whistles?

A. Carlin N. Morton.

Q. What renowned author of western stories chose Long Key as his favorite fishing ground?

A. Zane Grey.

Q. Who founded the Poetry Society of Florida?

A. Gilbert Maxwell.

Q. In what area did Rex Beach collect data for his novel *The Mating Call*?

A. Weekiwachee Springs.

Q. What well-known New York drama critic and author of American theatrical histories was born in Pensacola?

A. John Anderson.

Q. Where may a copy of Leonardo da Vinci's *The Last Supper* be seen reproduced in 300,000 mosaic tiles?

A. Masterpiece Gardens near Lake Wales.

Q. What newspaper became the first daily in the state in 1839?

A. The Apalachicola *Gazette*.

Q. Under President Franklin Roosevelt's Federal Music Project, who first conducted the Florida Symphony Orchestra?

A. John Bittner.

Q. What library houses the world's finest collection of books about Florida?

A. The P. K. Yonge Library of Florida History, University of Florida.

Q. What was the name of the first newspaper published in Florida in 1783?

A. *The East Florida Gazette,* in St. Augustine.

Q. What brought the end of the second newspaper published in Florida, which was published from July 14 until October 15, 1821?

A. The death of its editor, Richard W. Edes, of yellow fever.

Q. What noted black sculptor spent her childhood at Green Cove Springs?

A. Augusta Savage.

Q. Drawing from the rich history of the state, what author wrote two popular adventure novels, *Flamingo Feather* in 1887 and *The Coral Ship* in 1893?

A. Kirk Munroe.

Q. What three-day art and cultural extravaganza is held at Boynton Beach?

A. Boynton's G.A.L.A.

Q. What three-day art event featuring some of the nation's best artists is held at Walt Disney World Village?

A. Walt Disney World Festival of the Masters.

Q. What famous naturalist lived on Key West while he studied and painted native birds?

A. John James Audubon.

———◆———

Q. Palm Beach serves as a backdrop for what 1933 novel by Joseph Hergesheimer exploring the superficiality of those who work at play?

A. *Tropical Winter.*

———◆———

Q. What naturalist wrote such books as *In Lower Florida Wilds, Out of Doors in Florida,* and *Florida Wild Life* during the 1920s and 1930s?

A. Charles Torrey Simpson.

———◆———

Q. What event in Miami features cultural life during the Renaissance?

A. Fayre at Vizcaya.

———◆———

Q. The Friday Musicale, possibly the oldest music group in Florida, is headquartered in what city?

A. Jacksonville.

———◆———

Q. The University of Florida in Gainesville offers what popular facility for the production of theatrical performances?

A. The Hippodrome.

———◆———

Q. What Sarasota author created the popular Travis McGee novels?

A. John D. MacDonald.

Q. What theater executive and attorney born in Jacksonville joined the President's Advisory Cabinet in 1979?

A. John B. Kent.

Q. *Twelve Black Floridians,* by Leedell W. Neyland, was published by what institution in 1970?

A. Florida A&M University Foundation.

Q. Who was named Poet Laureate of Florida in 1980?

A. Edmund Skellings, Fort Lauderdale.

Q. How does the Miami Opera Company rank in size nationally?

A. Seventh.

Q. What noted Key West goldsmith's works have been applauded by fashion magazines?

A. John Buzogany.

Q. Where is the Stephen Foster Folk Culture Center?

A. White Springs.

Q. Famous landscape artist George Inness moved his home and studio to what Florida community in 1877?

A. Tarpon Springs.

Q. From her experience at Cross Creek, Marjorie Kinnan Rawlings wrote what Pulitzer Prize-winning novel?

A. *The Yearling.*

———◆———

Q. Noted "cowboy sculptor" Hughlette Wheeler, recognized for his animal figures, was born in what community?

A. Christmas.

———◆———

Q. What community was named for the home of Orlando poet Will Wallace Henry?

A. Pinecastle.

———◆———

Q. What 1923 Eugene O'Neill play was set in Florida and featured Ponce de León's search for the fountain of youth?

A. *The Fountain.*

———◆———

Q. Where was author Zora Neale Hurston's residence when she died?

A. The County Welfare Home at Fort Pierce.

———◆———

Q. For what novel did author MacKinlay Kantor win a 1956 Pulitzer Prize?

A. *Andersonville.*

———◆———

Q. Who was the first researcher to compile an extensive bibliography of books on Florida?

A. Daniel G. Brinton.

Q. What arts festival is the oldest and largest in northeastern Florida?

A. The River City Arts Festival in Jacksonville.

◆

Q. What was the title of the first brochure, printed in English in 1669, to promote real estate in Florida?

A. *A Brief Description of the Province on the Coasts of Florida.*

◆

Q. What Mandarin resident penned *Palmetto Leaves,* a series of sketches depicting the Reconstruction period following the Civil War?

A. Harriet Beecher Stowe.

◆

Q. The well-known New York architectural firm of Schulze and Weaver built the Waldorf-Astoria, the Los Angeles Biltmore, and what famous Palm Beach hotel?

A. The Breakers, 1925.

◆

Q. Hartley Toots Orchestra was well known in Miami in the 1930s for what type of music?

A. Swing.

◆

Q. What was the first newspaper published in Pensacola?

A. *The Floridian,* 1821–24.

◆

Q. When was the Monticello Opera House built?

A. 1890.

Q. While visiting Jacksonville in 1875, what noted Georgia poet was commissioned to create the first real tourist-oriented travel guide to the state of Florida, entitled *Florida, Its Scenery, Climate and History*?

A. Sidney Lanier.

◆

Q. What collection of colorful short stories and local Floridian customs was published in 1850 by Charles Lanman?

A. *Haw-Ho-Noo,* or *Records of a Tourist.*

◆

Q. In what Lilli B. McDuffee book is the Gamble mansion of Ellenton minutely described?

A. *The Lures of Manatee.*

◆

Q. What arts-related festival held in Winter Park is considered the most prestigious of its type in the Southeast?

A. The Sidewalk Art Festival.

◆

Q. Where is the renowned Asolo State Theater Company headquartered?

A. Sarasota.

◆

Q. What was the name of the first labor paper published in Tampa?

A. *El Internacional,* 1906.

◆

Q. What English-born composer started his career in Jacksonville in the mid-1880s?

A. Frederick Delius.

Q. What magazine writer, who became the third Mrs. Ernest Hemingway, met her future husband at Sloppy Joe's in Key West?

A. Martha Gellhorn.

◆

Q. Noted black writer James Weldon Johnson, known for such works as *Autobiography of an Ex-Colored Man* and *God's Trombones,* was born in what Florida city?

A. Jacksonville.

◆

Q. Who erected the Singing Tower at Mountain Lake?

A. Edward Bok.

◆

Q. Where is the Space Coast Art Festival held?

A. Cocoa Beach.

◆

Q. What museum houses one of the nation's best collections of Oriental bronzes?

A. Bass Museum, Miami Beach.

◆

Q. Key West was the birthplace of what famous primitive painter?

A. Mario Sanchez.

◆

Q. What event displaying the works of Florida's best artists is hosted by Rollins College?

A. Autumn Art Festival.

Q. Lantana is headquarters for what notorious tabloid newspaper?

A. *National Enquirer.*

———◆———

Q. Where is the Independent Film and Video Festival held?

A. Tampa.

———◆———

Q. April is the month for what musical event hosted by the Pioneer Florida Museum in Dade City?

A. Old Time Music Championship.

———◆———

Q. What writing team created the 1964 book exposing Florida's ecological situation, *Florida: Polluted Paradise?*

A. Hank Mesouf and June Cleo.

———◆———

Q. The former Florida Gulf Coast Symphony now performs under what name?

A. The Florida Orchestra (Tampa).

———◆———

Q. What jazz festival is held in late October in Clearwater?

A. Jazz Holiday.

———◆———

Q. Who created *Surrounded Islands,* an unusual avant-garde work of art, in Biscayne Bay in 1983?

A. Christo.

Q. How much do the bells in the Singing Tower weigh?

A. From approximately twelve pounds to eleven tons.

———◆———

Q. Who was the leader of the Sunset Royal Orchestra, the black swing band that worked out of West Palm Beach during the 1930s?

A. Ace Harris.

———◆———

Q. Stephen Crane, who came to international fame with his novel *The Red Badge of Courage,* wrote what acclaimed short story based on his shipwreck experience off the Florida coast in 1896?

A. "The Open Boat."

———◆———

Q. What author, in her 1927 work *Move Over,* chronicled the absurdities of the small talk of the wealthy in Palm Beach?

A. Ethel Pettit.

———◆———

Q. Stock Island is the location of what fine arts center named for an American playwright?

A. The Tennessee Williams Fine Arts Center.

———◆———

Q. What Pulitzer Prize-winning playwright wrote *Cross and Sword*?

A. Paul Green.

———◆———

Q. How did Stephen Foster choose the Suwannee River as the theme for his famous song?

A. He looked through an atlas for a southern river with "a good musical sound," which he modified for better euphony.

Q. Many buildings situated around Flamingo Park in Miami Beach are of what classic 1930s style?

A. Art deco.

———◆———

Q. What 1943 novel by Theodore Pratt, set in the southeastern part of Florida, was made into a movie?

A. *The Barefoot Mailman.*

———◆———

Q. For how many years did Ernest Hemingway live in Key West?

A. Ten.

———◆———

Q. Where is the Great Gulf Coast Arts Festival held each November?

A. Pensacola.

———◆———

Q. What Jacksonville-born entertainer/author wrote *Between You, Me and the Gatepost* in 1960 and *A New Song* in 1971?

A. Pat Boone.

———◆———

Q. Who organized the Symphony Society of Central Florida at Winter Park in 1926?

A. Mary Leonard.

———◆———

Q. Florida poet Gilbert Maxwell is best known for what collection of verse published in 1936?

A. *Stranger's Garment.*

Q. In 1860, what book on botany, still considered a standard, was published by Dr. Alvan Wentworth Chapman of Apalachicola?

A. *Flora of the Southern United States*.

◆

Q. The carillon of the Singing Tower contains how many bells?

A. Seventy-one.

◆

Q. Central Florida's only professional dance company performs under what name?

A. The Southern Ballet Theater.

◆

Q. Longtime *Miami Herald* crime reporter Edna Buchanan wrote what book of true tales of heinous crimes?

A. *The Corpse Had a Familiar Face*.

◆

Q. Who produced the 1973 pictorial study *The Everglades*?

A. Archie Carr.

◆

Q. White Springs is the home of what May festival?

A. The Florida Folk Festival.

◆

Q. Who founded the *Register,* the first Key West newspaper, in 1829?

A. Thomas Eastin.

Q. In what 1975 book did Tennessee Williams reflect on his life in Key West?

A. *Memoirs.*

———◆———

Q. Who wrote the 1928 novel *Strangers and Lovers,* dealing with a girl's fight against the harsh environment in the early days of Florida cattle country?

A. Edwin Granberry.

———◆———

Q. Wares produced by some of Florida's finest craftsmen may be enjoyed at what Lakeland fair?

A. Mayfaire-by-the-Lake.

———◆———

Q. What type of music is featured at the Sarasota Music Festival each June?

A. Chamber music.

———◆———

Q. What great American painter produced such works as *The Gulf Stream, Palms in the Storm, A Norther,* and *Taking on Wet Provisions,* during his visits to Key West in the 1890s?

A. Winslow Homer.

———◆———

Q. Ashley Gallery of Palm Beach specializes in art relating to what subject?

A. Sports, especially hunting.

———◆———

Q. What was the name of novelist Stephen Crane's wife, whom he met and married in Jacksonville?

A. Cora Taylor.

Q. What feature in the EPCOT Future World unfolds the development of art, music, drama, and literature?

A. Journey into Imagination.

◆

Q. What St. Petersburg afternoon newspaper has such confidence in the weather that it is given away free if the sun does not shine?

A. The *Evening Independent*.

◆

Q. What Coral Gables pioneer also was a noted photographer?

A. Ralph Middleton Munroe.

◆

Q. What is the University of Miami art museum named?

A. Lowe Art Museum.

◆

Q. What collection of historical Floridian photographs was published by Nixon Smiley in 1974?

A. *Yesterday's Florida*.

◆

Q. What is the main attraction at the Otter Springs Bluegrass Festival in Trenton?

A. Banjo picking.

◆

Q. What 1977 novel by John D. MacDonald portrays the effects of a hurricane on a cheaply constructed development in the Florida Keys?

A. *Condominium*.

ARTS & LITERATURE

Q. The annual Art in the Sun Festival is hosted by what community?

A. Pompano Beach.

Q. What eccentric nephew of Napoleon lived near Tallahassee and wrote *A Moral and Political Sketch of the United States of North America* in 1833?

A. Prince Achile Murat.

Q. What noted sculptor created the work *Collected Ghost Stories from the Work House,* situated on the campus of the University of South Florida?

A. Alice Aycock.

Q. Where was black novelist Zora Neale Hurston born?

A. Eatonville.

Q. What great American poet lived in Florida in 1827 to regain his health?

A. Ralph Waldo Emerson.

Q. In what year was the first building solely for staging theatrical performances erected in Jacksonville?

A. 1884.

Q. What newspaper ran more advertising linage than any other newspaper in the world from 1925 to 1926?

A. The *Miami Herald*.

Q. What artist produced a series of Seminole Indian portraits for the U.S. government in the late 1820s and early 1830s, including the portrait of Osceola?

A. George Catlin.

✦

Q. Where may John James Audubon's original Double Elephant folio of *Birds of America* be seen?

A. Audubon House, Key West.

✦

Q. Where in Miami is a Garden of the Blind where visitors can feel statuary and smell herbs and flowers?

A. Vizcaya Museum and Gardens.

✦

Q. What Florida author is noted for such works as *Fort Everglades*, *The Golden Isle*, and *In a Dark Garden*?

A. Frank Slaughter.

✦

Q. Who established the *Florida Intelligencer* in Tallahassee in 1825?

A. W. Hasell Hunt and Associates.

✦

Q. What is the only major opera company in the Southeast?

A. The Miami Opera Company.

✦

Q. What is the official Florida state song?

A. "Old Folks at Home."

Q. What novelist wrote *Maria*, *Don Juan McQueen*, and *Margaret's Story*, all set in Florida?

A. Eugenia Price.

———◆———

Q. In 1821, James Grant Forbes, noted author of the Florida territory, published what highly acclaimed book?

A. *Sketches of the History and Topography of Florida.*

———◆———

Q. Who authored *The Everglades: River of Grass*?

A. Marjory Stoneman Douglas, known as the "savior of the Everglades."

———◆———

Q. A major collection of works by Louis Comfort Tiffany can be found in what museum?

A. Charles Hosmer Morse Museum of American Art, Winter Park.

———◆———

Q. As a preservationist of Florida folk culture, for what is Thelma Boltin noted?

A. Storytelling.

———◆———

Q. What festival in Sarasota is a showcase of contemporary styles in American crafts?

A. The Ringling Crafts Festival.

———◆———

Q. Where is the Tampa Bay Bluegrass Festival held?

A. Riverview.

Q. The art festival Images is held in which community?

A. New Smyrna Beach.

———————◆———————

Q. Among what group of people are *Little Red Rabbit* and *Story of the Little Coon* musical classics?

A. The Seminole.

———————◆———————

Q. What musical event featuring a 141-voice choir accompanied by the Florida Symphony Orchestra takes place at Rollins College in February?

A. The Bach Festival of Winter Park.

———————◆———————

Q. What English naturalist collected and published prints of specimens of Florida plant life in 1731?

A. Mark Catesby.

———————◆———————

Q. What account of the flight of Confederate army officers and officials following the surrender of Lee at Appomattox was published in 1938 by Professor A. J. Hanna?

A. *Flight into Oblivion.*

———————◆———————

Q. What architect, noted for his work on Trinity Church in New York City, designed St. Marks Episcopal Church in Palatka about 1850?

A. Richard Upjohn.

———————◆———————

Q. What newspaper set a world's record for the largest single edition of a standard size newspaper on July 26, 1925, totaling 504 pages and weighing seven and one-half pounds?

A. The *Miami Daily News.*

Q. St. Petersburg hosts what type of musical groups each March?

A. All-American high school bands.

———◆———

Q. What St. Petersburg real estate developer and investment wizard wrote *This Was Florida's Boom*?

A. Walter Fuller.

———◆———

Q. What Florida author wrote *Jonah's Gourd Vine* in 1934 and *Their Eyes Were Watching God* in 1938?

A. Zora Neale Hurston.

———◆———

Q. What 1865 science fiction novel by Jules Verne was set in Bell Shoals?

A. *From the Earth to the Moon.*

———◆———

Q. What theatrical group erected a playhouse in Miami in 1929?

A. The Miami Civic Theater.

———◆———

Q. What 1937 novel by Ernest Hemingway contrasted the decadent, wealthy visitors to Key West with the island's local families?

A. *To Have and Have Not.*

———◆———

Q. What country-western composer penned a song about the Yeti-type creature from the Palatka area?

A. Billy Crain.

Q. A magnificent collection of the works of what famous Flemish painter is maintained in the Ringling collection?

A. Peter Paul Rubens.

———◆———

Q. Theodore Irving, Washington Irving's nephew, published what book in 1868 on de Soto's expedition?

A. *Conquest of Florida.*

———◆———

Q. What Hollywood arts festival features a mixture of music and visual arts?

A. The Seven Lively Arts Festival.

———◆———

Q. Who wrote the 1966 work *Frontier Eden: The Literary Career of Marjorie Kinnan Rawlings*?

A. Gordon E. Bigelow.

———◆———

Q. What renowned sculptor has a sculpture garden named in her honor at West Palm Beach?

A. Anne Norton.

———◆———

Q. What Florida poet won a Pulitzer Prize in 1932 for his collection of works entitled *The Flowering Stone*?

A. George Dillon.

———◆———

Q. The Brevard Art Center and Museum in Melbourne offers a gallery of touchable exhibits for what group of people?

A. The visually impaired.

Q. J. Rosamond Johnson of Jacksonville composed what song that became known as the black national anthem?

A. "Lift Every Voice and Sing."

———◆———

Q. In what city may the Las Olas Art Festival be enjoyed?

A. Fort Lauderdale.

———◆———

Q. Drawings by what French artist, who lived in Florida in 1564–65, are considered to be the first professional art produced by a European in America?

A. LeMoyne.

———◆———

Q. What composer wrote "Florida Rag" in 1905?

A. George L. Lowery.

———◆———

Q. What Indian tribe sponsors the Everglades Outdoors Music Festival?

A. The Miccosukee.

———◆———

Q. For whom is the library on the campus of the Bayboro Harbor extension of the University of South Florida named?

A. Noted St. Petersburg newspaperman Nelson Poynter.

———◆———

Q. The novel *The Dance of the Bends* by Eustace Adams is built around what subject matter?

A. Greek sponge fishers.

Q. Who wrote *How to Survive Your First Six Months in Florida and Love Every Minute of It*?

A. Robert W. Tolf.

Q. What is Florida's oldest library?

A. The St. Augustine Free Public Library opened in 1874.

Q. What January art show is held at Coral Gables?

A. Art Show on Miracle Mile.

Q. What Coconut Grove resident was noted for compiling and publishing classic poetry of the East in the 1920s?

A. Eunice Tietjens.

Q. In the early 1940s, what future playwright lived in Key West where he said he had a "love affair with a fishing village barely out of sight of Havana"?

A. Tennessee Williams.

Q. The Longwood Arts and Crafts Festival is centered around what restored historic house?

A. The Bradlee MacIntyre House.

Q. What Miami resident was best known for her songs "I Love Life," "Rachem," and "Nichavo"?

A. Mana-Zucca.

SPORTS & LEISURE

CHAPTER FIVE

Q. What annual football game is played between the Miami Police Department and the Metro-Dade County Deputy Dawgs?

A. The Pig Bowl.

———◆———

Q. What is the largest dog track in Florida?

A. Derby Lanes, St. Petersburg.

———◆———

Q. At what gym in Miami Beach did Muhammad Ali do some of his early training?

A. Chris Dundee's Fifth Street Gym.

———◆———

Q. Where does Florida rank nationally in the breeding of Thoroughbred horses?

A. Third.

———◆———

Q. In what museum can you learn about the greatest names in the circus world?

A. The Circus World of Fame, Sarasota.

Q. As of 1994, how many times has the University of Miami won the Orange Bowl?

A. Five (1946, 1984, 1988, 1989, 1992).

Q. What handball-type game was introduced to Florida from Cuba?

A. Jai alai.

Q. Flamingo Park in Miami Beach hosts what annual sporting event?

A. World Junior Tennis Championships.

Q. A saltwater all-tackle world's record was set in Daytona Beach in 1990 by catching what kind of fish weighing fifty pounds, eight ounces?

A. An African pompano.

Q. What eighteen-year veteran outfielder, born in Tampa, accepted a management position with the New York Yankees in 1986?

A. Louis ("Lou") Piniella.

Q. What water sport at Sebastian State Park brings large crowds of participants and spectators?

A. Surfing.

Q. How much does a nonresident fishing license cost for seven days?

A. $16.50.

Q. In 1964, what Florida Thoroughbred won the Kentucky Derby and the Preakness?

A. Carry Back.

———◆———

Q. What Tampa-born nineteen-year National League catcher became a brilliant American League manager?

A. Alfonso ("Al") Lopez.

———◆———

Q. Where is the Naval Aviation Museum?

A. Pensacola.

———◆———

Q. In 1972, what professional football team became the first team in NFL history to go through an entire season, including postseason games, unbeaten and untied?

A. The Miami Dolphins.

———◆———

Q. What has been called Palm Beach's "pet sport"?

A. Polo.

———◆———

Q. Florida is one of only three states in which pari-mutuel wagering is legal and operative for what sport?

A. Jai alai.

———◆———

Q. What Cleveland Indians pitcher was killed in 1993 in a boating accident during spring training in Winter Haven?

A. Steve Olin.

Q. Where was a saltwater all-tackle world's record set in 1982, by Allen Ogle maneuvering in a 99-pound great hammerhead shark?

A. Sarasota.

Q. What major league ball club conducts its March spring training in Vero Beach?

A. The Los Angeles Dodgers.

Q. How many Kentucky Derby champions has Florida produced as of 1993?

A. Five.

Q. Miami offers 138 miles of paved paths for participants in what leisurely pastime or sport?

A. Bicycling.

Q. What kind of racing is held at Tampa Track?

A. Greyhound.

Q. Zephyrhills near Tampa hosts what sporting event?

A. World parachuting championships.

Q. Where are the Busch Gardens situated?

A. Tampa.

Q. What Orlando native took the Men's Overall and the Men's Slalom at the forty-third Annual National Water Ski Championship?

A. Carl Robege.

———◆———

Q. A freshwater all-tackle world's record was set in 1981 at Boca Raton by catching what type of fish weighing twenty-one pounds, three ounces?

A. A Florida gar.

———◆———

Q. Miami is the home of what professional baseball team during spring training?

A. The Baltimore Orioles.

———◆———

Q. What county is said to have more golf courses than any other in the nation?

A. Palm Beach County.

———◆———

Q. The Miami Dolphins beat what team in the 1973 Super Bowl?

A. The Washington Redskins.

———◆———

Q. Where is the running of the Southern Ocean Racing Conference held each year?

A. St. Petersburg.

———◆———

Q. In what community is the Florida Championship Rodeo held?

A. Davie.

Q. What type of boat ride, not commonly found in the United States, is offered at the Villa Vizcaya, Miami?

A. Gondola.

Q. What championship bowling event is held at the Cloverleaf Lanes, North Miami Beach?

A. Bowling Tournament of the Americas.

Q. Born in Key West, what major league pitcher was signed to the Minnesota Twins in 1973?

A. Vic Albury.

Q. What community is known as "the World's Luckiest Fishing Village"?

A. Destin.

Q. What community gained fame by holding the world's largest barbecue?

A. New Port Richey.

Q. The Chicago White Sox are headquartered in what city during spring training?

A. Sarasota.

Q. NFL end Kenneth O. Burrough was born in what town?

A. Jacksonville.

Q. What is the largest hotel on Miami Beach?

A. The 1,224-room Fontainebleau Hilton.

———◆———

Q. What Tampa-born infielder played for the Kansas City Athletics, Oakland Athletics, Atlanta Braves, and Chicago Cubs?

A. Tony LaRussa.

———◆———

Q. What Florida community holds the title "Sailfish Capital of the World"?

A. Stuart.

———◆———

Q. What Tallahassee-born second baseman played in the major leagues eleven years, with a lifetime batting average of .248?

A. Jimmy Bloodworth.

———◆———

Q. How many land-speed records were set on Daytona Beach between 1902 and 1935?

A. Thirteen.

———◆———

Q. Situated on the west side of the Kissimmee airport, what museum displays World War II artifacts, along with plane exhibits?

A. Warbird Air Museum.

———◆———

Q. The annual Swamp Cabbage Festival is held in what Lake Okeechobee community?

A. Clewiston.

Q. What eccentric hotel is one of the most interesting attractions on Vero Beach?

A. The Driftwood Inn, built in 1932.

Q. Lakewood-born Bill White played what position for thirteen years with the New York Giants, San Francisco Giants, St. Louis Cardinals, and Philadelphia Phillies?

A. First baseman.

Q. What Orlando-born NFL player was all-pro and leading pass catcher in 1953, 1954, and 1955 with the Philadelphia Eagles?

A. Pete Pihos.

Q. What type of tribute is paid to Thomas Edison each February in Fort Myers?

A. The Pageant of Light.

Q. Dunedin is the home for what professional baseball team during spring training?

A. The Toronto Blue Jays.

Q. The *José Gasparilla*, docked on Bayshore Boulevard in Tampa, is what type of vessel?

A. A fully rigged pirate ship.

Q. Where is the Antique Car Meet, sponsored by the Birthplace of Speed Association, held each Thanksgiving?

A. Ormond Beach.

Q. The third Florida winner of the Kentucky Derby was what famous Thoroughbred?

A. Foolish Pleasure, 1975.

Q. "Key West bicycles" are noted for what unusual features?

A. Chest-high handlebars.

Q. What state park features a three-mile miniature railroad trip for visitors?

A. Hugh Taylor Birch State Park.

Q. Where is the world's largest domestic flock of flamingos maintained?

A. Hialeah Park.

Q. Where is the International Kite Flying Contest held?

A. Sarasota.

Q. As of 1993, how many times have the University of Miami Hurricanes been the number-one-ranked football team in the nation?

A. Four (1983, 1987, 1989, 1991).

Q. What Florida State University senior won the 1978 Metro Conference Basketball Player of the Year award?

A. Harry Davis.

Q. What running back won fifteen letters at Cocoa High School and went on to be consensus All-American while playing for Army in 1957?

A. Robert P. Anderson.

Q. What Miami Dolphins player was chosen the most valuable player of the 1973 Super Bowl?

A. Jake Scott.

Q. What is the only Thoroughbred track on Florida's west coast?

A. Tampa Bay Downs.

Q. The New York Yankees hold spring training in what city?

A. Fort Lauderdale.

Q. What World War II submarine may be toured in Tampa?

A. The USS *Requin*.

Q. What retired baseball pitcher ran a hunting lodge at Homosassa Springs?

A. Dazzy Vance.

Q. Where is the nation's largest youth baseball league?

A. Tamiami Park, Miami.

Q. Deer Island Pit on Lake San Susan was internationally known during the 1920s and 1930s for what activity?

A. Cock fighting.

Q. What baseball teams share West Palm Beach Municipal Stadium for their preseason spring training?

A. The Atlanta Braves and the Montreal Expos.

Q. Where is the Jefferson County Kennel Club?

A. Monticello.

Q. In what city is the annual AAU-sanctioned International Hall of Fame Diving Meet held?

A. Fort Lauderdale.

Q. In 1983, Larenza Mungin snagged the saltwater all-tackle world record for catching what type of fish at Nassau Sound?

A. A southern flounder, twenty pounds, nine ounces.

Q. What large mobile home tourist organization was formed at Tampa in 1920?

A. The Tin Car Tourists of the World.

Q. Where is the Rodeo Bowl situated?

A. Near Indiantown.

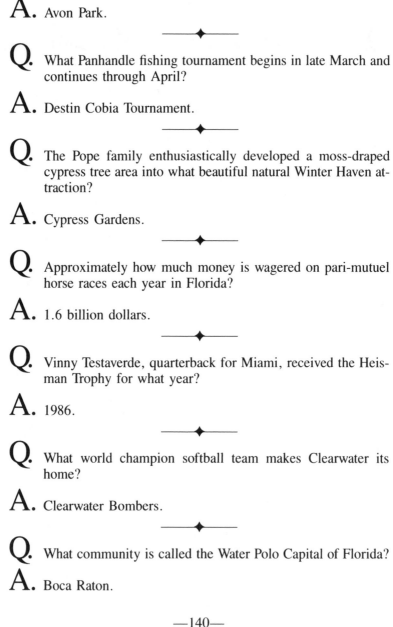

Q. Star outfielder and designated hitter for the Cincinnati Reds and the Kansas City Royals Hal McRae was born in what Florida community?

A. Avon Park.

Q. What Panhandle fishing tournament begins in late March and continues through April?

A. Destin Cobia Tournament.

Q. The Pope family enthusiastically developed a moss-draped cypress tree area into what beautiful natural Winter Haven attraction?

A. Cypress Gardens.

Q. Approximately how much money is wagered on pari-mutuel horse races each year in Florida?

A. 1.6 billion dollars.

Q. Vinny Testaverde, quarterback for Miami, received the Heisman Trophy for what year?

A. 1986.

Q. What world champion softball team makes Clearwater its home?

A. Clearwater Bombers.

Q. What community is called the Water Polo Capital of Florida?

A. Boca Raton.

Q. What Swamp Buggy track is situated in western Collier County?

A. Mile-o-Mud Track.

———◆———

Q. What marine attraction features an electric eel pavilion?

A. Marineland of Florida.

———◆———

Q. Where is the Venetian Pool situated?

A. Coral Gables.

———◆———

Q. What NFL team is headquartered in Tampa?

A. The Tampa Bay Buccaneers.

———◆———

Q. What major racing event is held each February at Daytona International Speedway?

A. The Daytona 500.

———◆———

Q. What sporting event on Panama City Beach is a qualifying race for the world championship Ironman Triathlon in Hawaii?

A. The Gulf Coast Triathlon.

———◆———

Q. Where is the annual Highland Games Festival held?

A. Dunedin.

Q. What St. Louis Cardinal pitcher, born in Miami, set a modern major league record in 1969 by striking out nineteen New York Mets?

A. Steve Carlton.

———◆———

Q. Lion Country Safari is in what county?

A. Palm Beach County.

———◆———

Q. What sports hall of fame is situated in West Palm Beach?

A. The Golf Hall of Fame.

———◆———

Q. What Florida city won the Polo United States Open against Retama?

A. Fort Lauderdale.

———◆———

Q. What University of Tampa athlete became known as "Mr. Wonderful" in wrestling circles?

A. Paul Orndorff.

———◆———

Q. On what type of racing are almost sixty-five million dollars wagered annually in Florida?

A. Greyhound.

———◆———

Q. What team opposed the Miami Dolphins in the 1985 Super Bowl?

A. The San Francisco 49ers.

Q. For what delicate dessert are the Florida Keys well known?

A. Key Lime Pie.

Q. What professional football team plays its practice games at Vero Beach during the months of July and August?

A. The New Orleans Saints.

Q. The Jacksonville class AA baseball team is a farm club of what major league team?

A. The Montreal Expos.

Q. What reptilian attraction first opened in St. Augustine in 1893?

A. The St. Augustine Alligator Farm.

Q. Where does the International Motor Sport Association conduct its annual championship finals?

A. Daytona International Speedway.

Q. What is the biggest blue marlin event on Florida's Gulf coast?

A. Marlin International Tournament, Destin.

Q. As of 1993, what driver has won the Daytona 500 seven times?

A. Richard Petty.

Q. Florida *claims* to have originated softball, which was first known by what name?

A. Diamond ball.

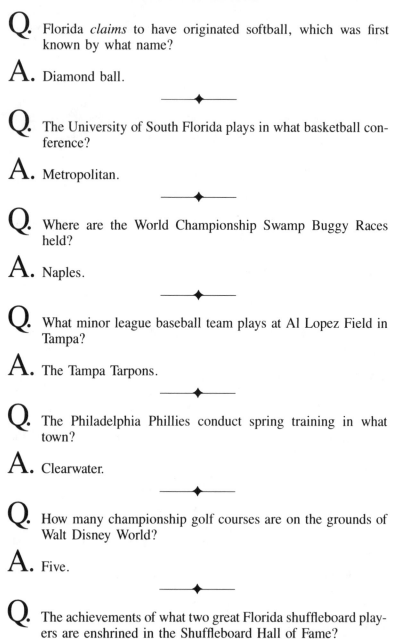

Q. The University of South Florida plays in what basketball conference?

A. Metropolitan.

Q. Where are the World Championship Swamp Buggy Races held?

A. Naples.

Q. What minor league baseball team plays at Al Lopez Field in Tampa?

A. The Tampa Tarpons.

Q. The Philadelphia Phillies conduct spring training in what town?

A. Clearwater.

Q. How many championship golf courses are on the grounds of Walt Disney World?

A. Five.

Q. The achievements of what two great Florida shuffleboard players are enshrined in the Shuffleboard Hall of Fame?

A. Lucy Perkins and Mae Hall.

Q. The Tampa Bay Bandits were members of what football league, 1983–85?

A. The United States Football League.

———✦———

Q. How many college students are estimated to visit Daytona Beach each year during spring break?

A. 300,000.

———✦———

Q. Who set the first recorded land speed record in 1902 at Ormond Beach at fifty-two miles per hour?

A. R. E. Olds and Alexander Winston.

———✦———

Q. The Hog's Breath 1,000, beginning in Miami and ending in Fort Walton Beach, is what type of race?

A. A world championship, long distance, one-design catamaran race.

———✦———

Q. Where in Tallahassee is a professional golf tournament held each April?

A. Killearn Country Club.

———✦———

Q. What is the nickname of the Key West High School football team?

A. "The Fighting Conchs."

———✦———

Q. The title of "Bass Fishing Capital of the World" is claimed by what town?

A. Palatka.

Q. The Swimming Hall of Fame Museum is in what city?

A. Fort Lauderdale.

◆

Q. What Miami Dolphins player set the all-time scoring record for the most points after touchdown in 1984?

A. Uwe von Schamann, with 66.

◆

Q. The official Women's Tennis Association Championships are held at what Florida location?

A. Amelia Island Plantation.

◆

Q. What horse racing track first brought the Miami area to national attention?

A. Hialeah Park.

◆

Q. What game of chance and superstition was brought to Tampa by Cubans in the 1880s?

A. Bolita.

◆

Q. What Florida A&M halfback, known as a great breakaway runner, played for the Chicago Bears from 1957 to 1963?

A. Willie Galimore.

◆

Q. Florida State University is a member of what football conference?

A. Atlantic Coast.

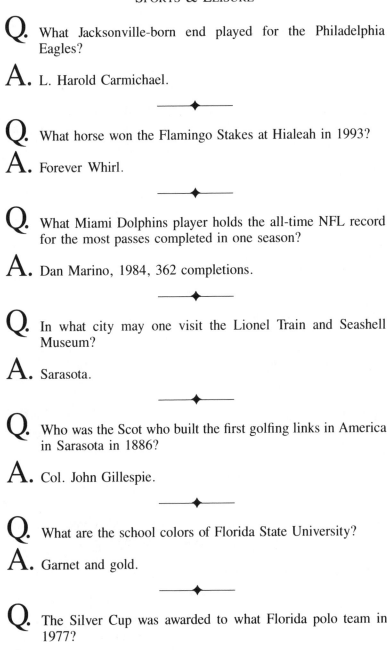

Q. What Jacksonville-born end played for the Philadelphia Eagles?

A. L. Harold Carmichael.

———◆———

Q. What horse won the Flamingo Stakes at Hialeah in 1993?

A. Forever Whirl.

———◆———

Q. What Miami Dolphins player holds the all-time NFL record for the most passes completed in one season?

A. Dan Marino, 1984, 362 completions.

———◆———

Q. In what city may one visit the Lionel Train and Seashell Museum?

A. Sarasota.

———◆———

Q. Who was the Scot who built the first golfing links in America in Sarasota in 1886?

A. Col. John Gillespie.

———◆———

Q. What are the school colors of Florida State University?

A. Garnet and gold.

———◆———

Q. The Silver Cup was awarded to what Florida polo team in 1977?

A. Boca Raton.

Q. Where is the Shuffleboard Hall of Fame located?

A. St. Petersburg.

◆

Q. Born in Winter Park, what Cincinnati Reds moundsman out-pitched Oakland's Catfish Hunter, Blue Moon Odom, and Vida Blue in the 1972 World Series?

A. John Eugene ("Jack") Billingham.

◆

Q. What golf course was frequented by John D. Rockefeller in his latter years?

A. The Ormond Beach Golf Links.

◆

Q. Where in Florida is it legal to play high-stakes bingo?

A. The Seminole Bingo Hall on the Federal Indian Reservation, Fort Lauderdale.

◆

Q. What Florida coach was selected the 1983 College Football Coach of the Year by the Football Writers Association of America?

A. Howard Schnellenberger, Miami.

◆

Q. What team won the 1985 Men's Church Slow Pitch, Amateur Softball Association National Championship?

A. Hickory Hammock, Milton.

◆

Q. Where was the 1976 saltwater all-tackle world's record set when Norton Thomton brought in a ninety-pound king mackeral?

A. Key West.

Q. In 1982, Tito Schnau caught what type of fish in Miami, weighing twenty-four pounds, eight ounces, and setting a world's record?

A. A horse-eye jack.

———◆———

Q. What special event highlights Okeechobee each Labor Day?

A. The Cattlemen's Association Rodeo.

———◆———

Q. Leading lifetime receiver Mark Clayton of Miami set what all-time NFL football record in 1984?

A. Most touchdown passes for one season, 18.

———◆———

Q. What is the seating capacity of the Orange Bowl stadium?

A. 74,712.

———◆———

Q. What race at Hialeah serves as a preparatory event for young horses aiming for the Kentucky Derby?

A. The Flamingo Stakes.

———◆———

Q. The George Halas Trophy for outstanding defensive play was awarded to what Tampa Bay player in 1979?

A. Lee Roy Selmon.

———◆———

Q. On October 28, 1979, what Miami-born ball player became manager of the New York Yankees?

A. Dick Howser.

Q. Who won the Heisman Trophy in 1992?

A. Gino Torretta, quarterback for the University of Miami.

———◆———

Q. Born in Apopka, what auto racer was the biggest money-winner in the history of stock car racing at his death in 1964?

A. Glenn ("Fireball") Roberts.

———◆———

Q. On what date is the Orange Bowl game played?

A. January 1.

———◆———

Q. Okeechobee is host for what annual festival?

A. The Speckled Perch Festival.

———◆———

Q. What Tampa-born Jefferson High athlete played twelve years as a pro for the Chicago Bears, Washington Redskins, and Miami Dolphins?

A. Ricardo ("Rick") Casares.

———◆———

Q. What is probably the most famous golf course in Dade County?

A. The Blue Monster at the Doral Country Club.

———◆———

Q. Who set the all-time NFL record in 1984 for the most rushing attempts in one season?

A. James Wilder, Tampa Bay Buccaneers, 407.

Q. What Miami Dolphins player received the Super Bowl MVP honors in 1974?

A. Larry Csonka.

———◆———

Q. Miami-born outfielder Mickey Rivers has played for what three clubs?

A. California Angels, New York Yankees, and Texas Rangers.

———◆———

Q. What outstanding baseball pitcher had his brilliant career placed in jeopardy in a hunting accident in 1964, while playing at Daytona Beach in the Florida State League?

A. Catfish Hunter.

———◆———

Q. What large hotel was the first built in Miami?

A. The Royal Palm.

———◆———

Q. First baseman Boog Powell, born in Lakeland, appeared in how many World Series?

A. Four (1966, 1969, 1970, and 1971, all with Baltimore).

———◆———

Q. Tinker Field in Orlando is spring training ground for what American League team?

A. The Minnesota Twins.

———◆———

Q. The Miami Dolphins lost to what team in the 1983 Super Bowl?

A. The Washington Redskins.

Q. What is the mechanical rabbit at greyhound racetracks called?

A. "Rusty."

———◆———

Q. What Jacksonville-born running back was named the *Sporting News* AFC Rookie of the Year in 1973?

A. Charles ("Boobie") Clark.

———◆———

Q. What Thoroughbred racetrack is situated north of Miami Beach near Hallandale?

A. Gulfstream Park.

———◆———

Q. Who set five land-speed records at Daytona Beach with his famous Bluebird?

A. Sir Malcolm Campbell.

———◆———

Q. The Pittsburgh Pirates take up residence in what community during spring training?

A. Bradenton.

———◆———

Q. What community is home for the Professional Golf Association headquarters?

A. Palm Beach.

———◆———

Q. Who was top scorer for the 1992–93 season for the Tampa Bay Lightning hockey team?

A. Brian Bradley.

Q. As of 1993, how many times was Miami Dolphins player Dan Marino the American Football Conference passing leader?

A. Four (1983, 1984, 1986, 1989).

Q. What nickname do fans call Florida Field?

A. "The Swamp."

Q. What is considered to be the Super Bowl of dog racing events?

A. The Hollywood International Classic.

Q. What Miami animal attraction has won international acclaim since it opened in 1981?

A. Metrozoo.

Q. What is the length of the annual canoe race on the Withlacoochee River?

A. Eighty-four miles.

Q. What top tournament event on the pro golf tour is held at Miami in late February or early March?

A. The Doral-Eastern Golf Open.

Q. Two 1985 Amateur Softball Association National Championship teams, the Key Ford Mustangs in Women's Major Slow Pitch and the Sheriff's Stars in Women's Industrial Slow Pitch, came from what Florida city?

A. Pensacola.

Q. The Charlotte County Stadium in Port Charlotte is home for what professional baseball team during spring training?

A. The Texas Rangers.

———◆———

Q. Lenny Faedo of the Minnesota Twins was born in what Florida city?

A. Tampa.

———◆———

Q. What minor league baseball team plays for the city of Orlando at Tinker Field?

A. The Orlando Cubs.

———◆———

Q. What hazardous sport is popular along the Santa Fe River?

A. Cave diving.

———◆———

Q. Alligatorland Safari is situated nine miles south of what town?

A. Kissimmee.

———◆———

Q. What Thoroughbred born and bred in Ocala won the Kentucky Derby in 1956?

A. Needles.

———◆———

Q. What major league baseball team makes St. Petersburg headquarters during spring training?

A. The St. Louis Cardinals.

Q. What entertainer first became a partner in the Miami Dolphin franchise secured in 1965?

A. Danny Thomas.

———◆———

Q. On what Florida Key does retired baseball great Ted Williams have a home?

A. Upper Matecumbe Key.

———◆———

Q. Orlando basketball enthusiasts are devoted to what professional team?

A. The NBA's Orlando Magic.

———◆———

Q. The Citrus Bowl is held in what city?

A. Orlando.

———◆———

Q. Miami is home for what NBA team?

A. Miami Heat.

———◆———

Q. Each year in mid-March, Sebring hosts what sporting event?

A. International Grand Prix Sports Car 12-Hour Endurance Race.

———◆———

Q. Where is the best surfing along Cocoa Beach?

A. Near the Canaveral Pier.

Q. What two consecutive years did the Miami Dolphins win the Super Bowl?

A. 1973 and 1974.

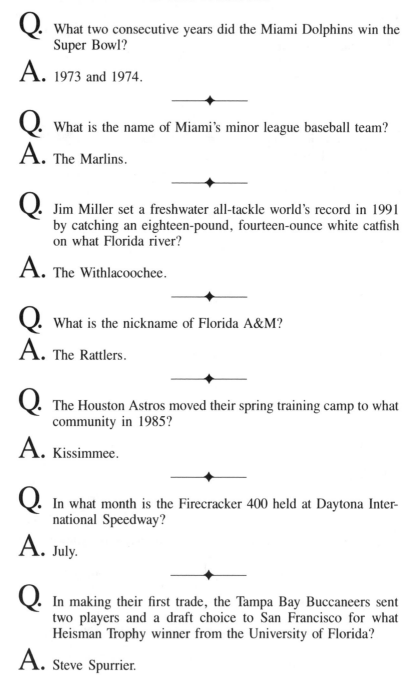

Q. What is the name of Miami's minor league baseball team?

A. The Marlins.

Q. Jim Miller set a freshwater all-tackle world's record in 1991 by catching an eighteen-pound, fourteen-ounce white catfish on what Florida river?

A. The Withlacoochee.

Q. What is the nickname of Florida A&M?

A. The Rattlers.

Q. The Houston Astros moved their spring training camp to what community in 1985?

A. Kissimmee.

Q. In what month is the Firecracker 400 held at Daytona International Speedway?

A. July.

Q. In making their first trade, the Tampa Bay Buccaneers sent two players and a draft choice to San Francisco for what Heisman Trophy winner from the University of Florida?

A. Steve Spurrier.

SCIENCE & NATURE

CHAPTER SIX

Q. What is the name of the 3,500-year-old, 138-foot-high cypress tree growing near Longwood?

A. The Senator.

———◆———

Q. What destroyed many of the sponge beds around Tarpon Springs in the 1940s?

A. Red tide (a proliferation of one-celled plantlike animals).

———◆———

Q. In what year did Cape Canaveral launch its first manned suborbital space flight?

A. 1961.

———◆———

Q. What ocean current runs close to the shores of Panama City Beach?

A. The Yucatan Current, part of the Gulf Stream.

———◆———

Q. What zoo houses the largest display of parrots in the world?

A. Busch Gardens, Tampa.

Q. What is the Florida state freshwater mammal?

A. The manatee.

Q. By what name are tornadoes called along coastal communities?

A. Waterspouts.

Q. What was the first space shuttle to be launched from the Kennedy Space Center?

A. *Columbia*.

Q. What type of product may be extracted and processed from the seed of the sago palm?

A. High quality starch.

Q. In what type of leaves did early settlers wrap cuts of meat to tenderize them?

A. Papaya leaves.

Q. Where are the most important deposits of Pleistocene era fossils in Florida?

A. The Melbourne bone beds along the east coast.

Q. What rare hawk is found in coastal areas and the southern part of Florida?

A. Short-tailed hawk.

Q. What instrument was used in early days to communicate between islands in the Florida Keys?

A. Conch shell horns.

———◆———

Q. What name is given to cow ponies that are descendants of early Spanish stock?

A. Marshtackies.

———◆———

Q. For what citrus fruit are the Florida Keys best known?

A. Limes.

———◆———

Q. Where was the tangelo first hybridized?

A. University of Florida's Subtropical Experimental Station, Homestead.

———◆———

Q. The St. Lucie Nuclear Power Plant is on what island?

A. Hutchinson Island.

———◆———

Q. What type of works was established by the Confederates in 1862 at Panama City?

A. A salt works to extract salt from seawater.

———◆———

Q. What is the average annual rainfall for Florida?

A. Fifty-three inches.

Q. What is the Florida state bird?

A. Mockingbird.

◆

Q. Where is Space Congress held?

A. Cocoa Beach.

◆

Q. What fraction of the nation's oranges and grapefruits are produced in Florida?

A. About three-fourths.

◆

Q. Xanadu, "the home of the future" built at Orlando in 1983, is made of what material?

A. Plastic foam.

◆

Q. What type of concretions are found in deposits at Ballast Point?

A. Geodes (small, hollow spheroidal rocks with crystals lining the inside wall).

◆

Q. Shark liver oil is high in what vitamin?

A. Vitamin A.

◆

Q. While working for the British Admiralty near Lake Louisa in 1917, Charles Lindly-Wood discovered a large deposit of what material utilized in various industrial manufacturing applications?

A. Diatomite.

Q. Who became the first American woman in space when launched from the Kennedy Space Center?

A. Sally K. Ride.

———◆———

Q. The Florida Trail offers how many miles of hiking trails?

A. More than 950.

———◆———

Q. What color are Spanish moss flowers?

A. Yellow-green.

———◆———

Q. Turtle Mound, which rises thirty-five feet on the east coast, is comprised of what material?

A. Oyster shells.

———◆———

Q. Where is Houser's Zoo situated?

A. Melbourne.

———◆———

Q. What flowering shrub is found exclusively in the wild in the pinelands of the western part of Florida?

A. Chapman's rhododendron.

———◆———

Q. What is the process called in which the bark of pine trees is scraped off to secure turpentine gums?

A. Bleeding.

Q. What is the weight of a cubic foot of black ironwood, native to Florida?

A. Eighty-one pounds.

Q. What are the dried tops, or vines, of peanut plants called when used as livestock feed?

A. Peanut hay.

Q. Forests cover what fraction of Florida?

A. About one-half.

Q. What is the Florida state saltwater mammal?

A. The dolphin.

Q. What purple-flowered, floating water plant often impedes navigation on lakes and streams in Florida?

A. Water hyacinth.

Q. In harvesting sap from pine trees for turpentine distillery operations, what is termed a "crop"?

A. Approximately 250 acres.

Q. Who founded the Reptile Institute at Silver Springs?

A. Ross Allen.

Q. On what Florida Key does Sea World maintain the Shark Institute?

A. Long Key.

———◆———

Q. What famous French marine explorer produced a television special about the endangered manatees?

A. Jacques Cousteau.

———◆———

Q. Known as one of the best shell-collecting areas in the state, Sanibel Island hosts what event in March?

A. Sanibel Shell Fair.

———◆———

Q. Approximately how many varieties of fish live in the Everglades?

A. About 600.

———◆———

Q. What tree near Orange Springs reaches thirty-two feet in height and is the largest of its kind in the United States?

A. Pinckneya.

———◆———

Q. How many varieties of palms are native to Florida?

A. Fifteen.

———◆———

Q. What unusual creature native to Southeast Asia has become quite common along the eastern coast and the central section of Florida since its escape to the wilds in the early 1960s?

A. The walking catfish.

Q. By what other name is the endangered osprey known?

A. Fish hawk.

◆

Q. Through tests at Thomas Edison's Botanical Research Corporation in Fort Myers, what plant did Edison discover to be a practical source of processed rubber?

A. Goldenrod.

◆

Q. The once-endangered wood duck, now plentiful in the state, seeks what type of nesting accommodations?

A. Natural tree cavities.

◆

Q. What is the Florida state flower?

A. Orange blossom.

◆

Q. What museum features a real iceberg and enables its visitors to experience the effects of a hurricane?

A. Planet Ocean, Miami.

◆

Q. What is the average annual temperature of Key West?

A. 74.4 degrees.

◆

Q. What is the most valuable truck crop in Florida?

A. Tomatoes.

SCIENCE & NATURE

Q. Although birds may be seen wading a mile from shore in shallow Lake Okeechobee, what is its greatest depth?

A. Twenty-four feet.

———◆———

Q. Who was the Kansas cattleman who greatly improved Florida beef stock by importing Brahma bulls from India during the 1860s?

A. E. E. Goodno.

———◆———

Q. What is the Florida state saltwater fish?

A. Atlantic sailfish.

———◆———

Q. What river is considered to be the last wild river in the southeastern part of Florida?

A. The Loxahatchee River.

———◆———

Q. What is the total area of the Vehicle Assembly Building at the Kennedy Space Center?

A. 129.5 million square feet.

———◆———

Q. What is Florida's official gemstone?

A. Moonstone.

———◆———

Q. What wildlife area adjoins the John F. Kennedy Space Center?

A. The Merritt Island National Wildlife Refuge.

Q. The notorious 1935 Labor Day hurricane with 200 m.p.h. winds set what new U.S. Weather Bureau record?

A. Lowest barometric pressure reading at sea level, 26.35 inches.

---◆---

Q. The hard wood of what type of tree in the Florida Keys was used in the manufacture of bowling balls?

A. Silver-barked lignum vitae.

---◆---

Q. What is the most common variety of tree in Florida?

A. Pine.

---◆---

Q. Gadsden and Marion counties produce what mineral used in petroleum refinement?

A. Fuller's earth.

---◆---

Q. Florida supplies the nation with 60 percent of what type of fish?

A. Red snapper.

---◆---

Q. The largest red mangrove in the United States is found in what national park?

A. Everglades National Park.

---◆---

Q. What city is the home of the Museum of Science and Space Transit Planetarium?

A. Miami.

Q. What is the southernmost key on which fresh water may be obtained by drilling?

A. Key Vaca.

———◆———

Q. The southern keys from Bahia Honda Key to the Dry Tortugas are comprised of what type of material?

A. White oölitic limestone.

———◆———

Q. What sea turtle has a pelican-like pouch?

A. The trunk turtle.

———◆———

Q. What is the name of the impressive coastal soaring bird noted for its ninety-inch wingspan?

A. Magnificent frigate bird.

———◆———

Q. What is the name of the native building rock composed of hard shells that has been mined in Flagler, St. Johns, and Volusia counties?

A. Coquina.

———◆———

Q. What is Florida's leading cash crop?

A. Oranges.

———◆———

Q. In what year was the first space shuttle launched from Kennedy Space Center?

A. 1981.

Q. What two native palm varieties have pinnate, or feather, leaves?

A. The royal and coconut palms.

Q. What institute in Melbourne maintains a botanical garden with more than 300 varieties of tropical foliage?

A. The Florida Institute of Technology.

Q. What are the three most common marine grasses in Florida?

A. Eel, turtle, and manatee varieties.

Q. What archeologist financed and directed extensive investigations into the shell and sand mounds of Florida in the 1890s?

A. Clarence Bloomfield Moore.

Q. How many square miles does the Big Cypress Swamp cover?

A. 2,400.

Q. Spanish moss receives all of its nourishment from what source?

A. The air.

Q. By what name are Florida land tortoises called?

A. Gophers.

Q. What international body officially proclaimed the Everglades a World Heritage Site in 1979, putting it in the company of the Serengeti Plain in Africa, Mount Everest, and the Galápagos Islands?

A. The United Nations.

———◆———

Q. What do frog farmers call frog legs?

A. Saddles.

———◆———

Q. What commercial use was found for processed Spanish moss?

A. As stuffing for mattresses and upholstery.

———◆———

Q. What space shuttle exploded seventy-three seconds into its flight on January 28, 1986, bringing about a reevaluation of the nation's space program?

A. *Challenger.*

———◆———

Q. Dr. Thunder's Magic Boom Room in the Museum of Science and Industry in Tampa simulates what natural phenomenon?

A. A Florida thunderstorm.

———◆———

Q. What is the most prevalent tall grass found in the Everglades?

A. Sawgrass.

———◆———

Q. Quick-growing slash and loblolly pine trees supply raw material for what Florida industry?

A. The paper industry.

Q. What natural event destroyed large areas of citrus trees in 1894–95?

A. A severe freeze.

Q. Florida has been unofficially called the nation's "capital" for what type of dangerous natural phenomenon?

A. Lightning.

Q. By what other name is the pompano fish known?

A. Butterfish.

Q. What mineral is mined from the Bone Valley gravel deposits in the Bartow region?

A. Pebble phosphate.

Q. The Everglades cover how many square miles?

A. 2,746 square miles (7,112 square kilometers).

Q. Who brought limes from the Yucatan Peninsula and transplanted them to the Florida Keys?

A. Dr. Henry E. Perrine.

Q. What is the Florida state seashell?

A. Horse conch, *Pleuroplaca giganta*.

Q. What group introduced St. Augustine creeper grass to Florida by way of seed carried in hay fodder for their livestock?

A. The Spanish.

———◆———

Q. The largest loblolly-bay tree in the nation is in what national forest?

A. Ocala National Forest.

———◆———

Q. Apalachicola Bay produces 90 percent of Florida's total production of what shellfish?

A. Oysters.

———◆———

Q. What type of wells that flow on the same principle as springs are common in certain areas of Florida?

A. Artesian.

———◆———

Q. What is the name of the supposed Sasquatch-like creature that is said to inhabit the woods around Palatka?

A. The Booger.

———◆———

Q. What is the normal operating speed of the giant crawler-transporter that carries rockets to their launch sites at Kennedy Space Center?

A. One mile per hour.

———◆———

Q. Who founded the Suncoast Seabird Sanctuary at Indian Shores?

A. Dr. Ralph Heath, Jr.

Q. What is the official Florida state stone?

A. Agatized coral.

———◆———

Q. What area is noted for having the largest concentration of orchids native to North America?

A. Fakahatchee Straud in Collier County.

———◆———

Q. During their mating season, what black insects are commonly killed on windshields and fronts of vehicles?

A. Lovebugs (bibinoid flies).

———◆———

Q. The waters of the John Pennekamp Coral Reef State Park offer a view of how many varieties of coral?

A. Forty-one.

———◆———

Q. What is the temperature of Warm Mineral Springs?

A. Eighty-seven degrees.

———◆———

Q. What National Wildlife Refuge is situated off the Gulf coast between Port St. Joe and Apalachicola?

A. St. Vincent Island.

———◆———

Q. In what direction does a flamingo normally turn its head when feeding?

A. Upside down.

Q. A search for what item first brought Thomas Alva Edison to Fort Myers in 1886?

A. A suitable filament for his incandescent lamp.

———◆———

Q. Who donated 2,200 acres to the U.S. Department of Agriculture in 1932 for the establishment of the Chinsegut Hill Sanctuary?

A. Col. Raymond Robins.

———◆———

Q. What was the name of the United States' first earth satellite launched from Cape Canaveral in 1958?

A. *Explorer I.*

———◆———

Q. Florida annually produces about 170 million pounds of what nut?

A. Peanuts.

———◆———

Q. What is Florida's most abundant mineral?

A. Limestone.

———◆———

Q. What is tabby?

A. An early building material made of oyster shells and lime, prevalent along the coast.

———◆———

Q. What is the only type of palm that grows naturally throughout Florida?

A. Cabbage palmetto.

Q. What park in the Miami area was built with specific activities and facilities for the handicapped?

A. Bird Drive Park and Therapeutic Campground.

Q. In the spring, what type of bird migrates to Bush Key to nest from as far away as West Africa?

A. The sooty tern.

Q. The name *Everglades* is a corruption of what early name for the area?

A. River Glades.

Q. What do the letters in EPCOT represent?

A. Experimental Prototype Community of Tomorrow.

Q. What is Palm Beach County's largest cash crop?

A. Sugar cane.

Q. What type of animal appears in more varieties in Florida than in any other state?

A. Fish.

Q. The Edison Home Museum, featuring some of Thomas Edison's early inventions, may be seen in what city?

A. Fort Myers.

Science & Nature

Q. What large marine creature weighing two tons and measuring thirty feet across did President Theodore Roosevelt land near Captiva Island on a small key?

A. A giant manta ray, or devilfish.

———◆———

Q. What type of clay, found primarily in Lake and Putnam counties, is used to produce fine china?

A. Kaolin.

———◆———

Q. Florida ranks first in the production of what natural sweetener?

A. Honey.

———◆———

Q. Because of the porous nature of the limestone that underlies much of Florida, what geological formation often appears when the water table drops?

A. Sinkhole.

———◆———

Q. What two crustaceans account for more than half of the seafood industry in Florida?

A. Shrimp and lobster.

———◆———

Q. The Santa Fe River is a tributary of what river?

A. The Suwannee.

———◆———

Q. What is the common thatching material the Seminole Indians utilized in roofing their huts?

A. Palmetto leaves.

Q. What was the first national forest organized in the eastern states?

A. Ocala (1908).

Q. Homestead is the location of what commercial attraction featuring hundreds of varieties of orchids?

A. Orchid Jungle.

Q. In the Ten Thousand Islands area, what do local residents call a variety of oyster that clings to mangrove roots and is exposed above water at low tide?

A. Coon oysters, which are relished by raccoons.

Q. What tree imported from China is cultivated for the oil extracted from the nuts it produces for use in wood finishes?

A. Tung.

Q. What is the daily output of Silver Springs?

A. Eight hundred million gallons of water per day.

Q. What rare yucca tree grows along the Apalachicola River west of Tallahassee?

A. Torrey yucca.

Q. Diatomite, which appears in Polk, Lake, and Santa Rosa counties, is composed of what type of fossil remains?

A. Microscopic marine plants.

Q. What prehistoric items are harvested at Venice with a "snow shovel" invented for that purpose?

A. Shark teeth.

———◆———

Q. What rare hawk-like bird from South America may be seen around Lake Okeechobee and the Loxahatchee Refuge?

A. Snail kite.

———◆———

Q. A mixture of what materials was used to plaster the walls of the Gamble mansion at Ellenton during construction between 1842 and 1845?

A. Lime, sand, and sugar.

———◆———

Q. What farm is the state's largest producer of Chinese vegetables?

A. Sang Yick Farm near Hobe Sound.

———◆———

Q. During what months do most citrus trees bloom?

A. From early March through June.

———◆———

Q. What is the first stage in the development of a hurricane?

A. A tropical disturbance.

———◆———

Q. A paste made from the roots of what wild plant was used by early farmers to rid fields of crows and to help keep away flies and mosquitoes?

A. Osceola's plume, or crow-poison.

Q. What federal agency provides hurricane information and warnings?

A. The National Hurricane Center in Miami.

Q. Tampa limestone is used in the manufacture of what product?

A. Cement.

Q. At what speed does water flow through the Everglades?

A. About one-half mile per day.

Q. In 1927, a singing contest was conducted near Lake Wales at Bok Tower between what two types of birds?

A. A mockingbird and a European nightingale.

Q. The largest cabbage palmetto in the nation, as recorded by the American Forestry Association, is found in what Florida park?

A. Highlands Hammock State Park.

Q. What cemetery is noted for recycling its graves to make room for newcomers?

A. City Cemetery in Key West.

Q. Three million dollars' worth of what illegal substance was burned at one time at the Port Everglades plant of the Florida Power and Light Company?

A. Marijuana.

Q. What is the average height of the miniature Key deer?

A. Twenty-six to thirty-two inches.

Q. What has shrimp been labeled by commercial shrimpers along the Gulf coast?

A. "Pink gold."

Q. How many different kinds of trees are found in Florida?

A. More than 360.

Q. What wading bird is known for its wailing night cry and hobbling walk?

A. Limpkin.

Q. What four poisonous snakes are indigenous to Florida?

A. Rattlesnake, cottonmouth, copperhead, and coral snake.

Q. What substance, eroded from the Appalachian Mountains, now comprises the sand on Amelia Island?

A. Quartzite.

Q. Now almost exclusively found in Florida, what endangered animals inspired the legend of mermaids?

A. Manatees.

Q. What animal product was much prized by rural settlers for soothing stiff joints and arthritis?

A. Panther oil.

Q. Who was the distinguished pioneer in the study of subtropical plants who was killed by Indians on Indian Key in 1840?

A. Dr. Henry Perrine.

Q. Visitors to Sanibel Island spend so much time combing the beaches for shells that they develop what condition?

A. "Sanibel stoop."

Q. Florida has the largest deposits of what mineral in the United States?

A. Phosphate.

Q. What is the Florida state freshwater fish?

A. Largemouth bass.

Q. A staple food of the Seminole Indians called *sofkee* is a mush made from what ground grain?

A. Corn.

Q. For what two items did Ponce de León search in Florida?

A. Gold and the regenerative fountain of youth.

Q. What is the Florida state tree?

A. The Sabal palm.

———◆———

Q. What two types of pelicans may be seen in Florida?

A. The American white pelican and the brown pelican.

———◆———

Q. What is the largest remaining subtropical wilderness in the continental United States?

A. The Everglades National Park.

———◆———

Q. What early term was applied to gummy products derived from pine tree rosin for caulking wooden ships?

A. Naval stores.

———◆———

Q. Where does Florida rank among states in the production of grapefruit?

A. First.

———◆———

Q. Indians marked trees in a five-mile circle around what spring, designating it as a safe area in which wounded warriors could recuperate?

A. White Springs.

———◆———

Q. Water from what river was sought after in the 1700s because of the high acid content that enabled lengthy storage in casks?

A. St. Marys River.

Q. What Florida fruit was noted by French botanist André Michaux in 1778 as "the glorified melon that climbed a tree"?

A. The papaya.

✦

Q. Hutchinson Island is best known for what activity that occurs from May to September?

A. Sea turtle nesting.

✦

Q. What river vanishes underground for a short distance at the Natural Bridge southeast of Tallahassee?

A. St. Marks River.

✦

Q. What is the most common disease of grapefruit?

A. Melanose.

✦

Q. The fossil remains of what creature were removed from Wakulla Springs and displayed at the state Geological Survey Museum?

A. Mastodon.

✦

Q. From what spring did President Grover Cleveland have water shipped regularly to Washington, DC, for use in the White House?

A. Magnolia Springs.

✦

Q. What variety of nut introduced to Florida from Mexico by John Hunt of Bagdad won honors at the 1873 Paris Exposition?

A. Turkey egg pecan.

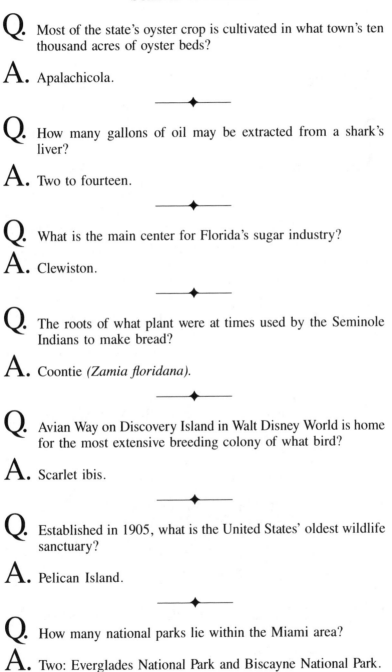

Q. Most of the state's oyster crop is cultivated in what town's ten thousand acres of oyster beds?

A. Apalachicola.

Q. How many gallons of oil may be extracted from a shark's liver?

A. Two to fourteen.

Q. What is the main center for Florida's sugar industry?

A. Clewiston.

Q. The roots of what plant were at times used by the Seminole Indians to make bread?

A. Coontie *(Zamia floridana)*.

Q. Avian Way on Discovery Island in Walt Disney World is home for the most extensive breeding colony of what bird?

A. Scarlet ibis.

Q. Established in 1905, what is the United States' oldest wildlife sanctuary?

A. Pelican Island.

Q. How many national parks lie within the Miami area?

A. Two: Everglades National Park and Biscayne National Park.

Q. On what island is the J. N. ("Ding") Darling National Wildlife Refuge?

A. Sanibel Island.

Q. A grouping of how many springs comprises Silver Springs?

A. 150.

Q. What land-building tree is found in three varieties in Florida?

A. Mangrove.

Q. What state park ranks as Florida's most popular?

A. Sebastian.

Q. What is Florida's most commercially valuable crustacean?

A. Shrimp.

Q. What type of tree in Jessie Ball du Pont Park in Jacksonville is considered to be the state's oldest on the east coast?

A. An oak, approximately 800 years old.

Q. Beachgoers are at times tormented by what dark-brown, hairy, small insect?

A. The sand fly.

Q. What is Florida's largest forest?

A. Blackwater River State Forest.

———◆———

Q. What large sinkhole near Gainesville covers five acres and drops to a depth of one hundred feet?

A. The Devil's Millhopper.

———◆———

Q. What group was instrumental in the establishment of the Corkscrew Swamp Sanctuary in 1954?

A. The Audubon Society.

———◆———

Q. By what other name are cockroaches called in Florida?

A. Palmetto bugs.

———◆———

Q. What disease is decimating the coconut palm population?

A. Lethal yellowing.

———◆———

Q. What state park surrounds a living coral reef?

A. John Pennekamp Coral Reef State Park.

———◆———

Q. What trees are the most valuable commercially in Florida?

A. Slash pine.

Q. Flocks of what Old World species of bird may commonly be seen feeding in pastures?

A. Cattle egret.

◆

Q. What type of destructive tropical storms, usually generated in the Caribbean Sea, at times buffet coastal communities?

A. Hurricanes.

◆

Q. How many tons of solids are carried off in solution each day at Rainbow Springs?

A. Six hundred.

◆

Q. A shark's mouth may contain up to how many rows of teeth?

A. Nineteen.

◆

Q. What two types of vultures are common to Florida?

A. Turkey vulture and black vulture.

◆

Q. An area off the Florida-Georgia coast has been determined to be the birthing grounds of what endangered marine mammal?

A. Right whales *(Balaena glacialis)*.

◆

Q. What is the leading food product processed in Florida?

A. Citrus fruit.

Q. What plant was introduced to the southern part of Florida during World War I in hopes of processing oil from it for use in airplane engines?

A. Castor bean.

———————◆———————

Q. What western predator is now common in the Panhandle and northern portion of Florida?

A. The coyote.

———————◆———————

Q. What colorful snail is found in the Everglades?

A. *Liguus* snail.

———————◆———————

Q. In what community is the largest cajeput tree growing, reaching a height of eighty-three feet?

A. Davie.

———————◆———————

Q. What is the gestation period of the Florida panther?

A. Ninety days.

———————◆———————

Q. Originally from Australia, what common household bird is now well established in the wilds around the St. Petersburg area?

A. Budgerigar, commonly called parakeet.

———————◆———————

Q. The Marie Selby Botanical Gardens, featuring fourteen acres of rare and exotic plants, is in what city?

A. Sarasota.

Q. What uncommon long-legged scavenger bird in Florida receives its name from its call?

A. Crested caracara.

———◆———

Q. Approximately how thick is the layer of marine-laid limestone that rests upon the foundation rock layers of Florida?

A. Approximately 4,000 feet.

———◆———

Q. What large reptile is found only in brackish, or salty, water in the southern extremities of Florida?

A. The rare American crocodile.

———◆———

Q. What European fruit scourge was discovered in the Orlando area in 1929?

A. The Mediterranean fruit fly.

———◆———

Q. What colorful wading bird is at home walking about on lily pads?

A. Purple gallinule.

———◆———

Q. Crushed seeds from what tree were sprinkled in inlets and streams by early settlers on Little and Middle Torch keys to stupefy fish for easy gathering?

A. Soapberry tree.

———◆———

Q. What plant cultivated by the early English colonists was used to obtain dye?

A. Indigo.

Q. The underdeveloped upper Florida Keys are the result of thousands of years of construction by what tiny animals?

A. Coral.

———◆———

Q. Roosting towers were built in the 1920s in the keys in the Hillsborough Road area for what type of creatures?

A. Bats.

———◆———

Q. What saltwater fish is of great commercial value in the production of fertilizer and for the oil that it produces?

A. Menhaden.

———◆———

Q. What is the name of the Key Biscayne Zoo, which features more than one thousand birds, animals, and reptiles?

A. Cradon Park Zoo.

———◆———

Q. The white-to-cream-colored Ocala limestone occasionally contains what type of vertebrate sea mammal fossils?

A. Zeuglodon, an early ancestor of the whale.

———◆———

Q. What town is known as the Home of the Tangerine?

A. Brooksville.

———◆———

Q. What is Florida's most valuable field crop?

A. Sugar cane.

Q. What is the name of the world's largest environmental test chamber, located at Eglin Air Force Base?

A. The McKinley Climatic Laboratory.

———◆———

Q. What flat-billed pink wading bird almost became extinct in Florida?

A. Roseate spoonbill.

———◆———

Q. What did the Indians call the seed of the yellow lotus?

A. *Hatchee* ("water") *chinquapin*.

———◆———

Q. What type of rock represents the oldest exposed sedimentary rock in Florida?

A. Ocala limestone from the Eocene epoch.

———◆———

Q. The Gulf Stream comes closest to the Florida shore at what location?

A. Boca Raton.

———◆———

Q. During which era does *Equus,* the prehistoric one-toed horse, appear in Florida deposits?

A. Pleistocene.

———◆———

Q. In which city is the Alexander Brest Planetarium situated?

A. Jacksonville.

SCIENCE & NATURE

Q. What wildlife refuge is in Sarasota County?

A. Myakka River State Park.

———◆———

Q. What common swamp-dwelling tree is noted for its buttressed trunk and unique "knees"?

A. Cypress.

———◆———

Q. What was the name of the scarlet dye pressed by the English from insects commonly found on east coast cacti?

A. Cochineal.

———◆———

Q. What city is known as the Gladioli Capital of the World?

A. Fort Myers.

———◆———

Q. How many varieties of terrestrial orchids are there in the state?

A. Sixty-four.

———◆———

Q. What is the name of the largest tropical botanical garden in the continental United States?

A. Fairchild Tropical Gardens, in Coral Gables.

———◆———

Q. What Florida lake is the second largest natural body of fresh water completely in the United States?

A. Lake Okeechobee (Lake Michigan is first).